MW00426974

GOD'S WISDOM IS BETTER THAN GOLD

"HOW MUCH BETTER IT IS
TO GET WISDOM THAN GOLD!"
PROVERBS 16:16

ADRIAN ROGERS

innovo
PUBLISHING
innovopublishing.com

Published by Innovo Publishing, LLC
www.innovopublishing.com
1-888-546-2111

Providing Full-Service Publishing Services for Christian Authors, Artists &
Ministries: Hardbacks, Paperbacks, eBooks, Audiobooks, Music, Screenplays
& Curricula

God's Wisdom Is Better than Gold

ISBN: 978-1-61314-156-4

Cover Design & Interior Layout: Innovo Publishing, LLC

Printed in the United States of America
U.S. Printing History
First Edition: 2021

Has God called you to create a Christian book, eBook, audiobook, music album,
screenplay, film, or curricula? If so, visit the ChristianPublishingPortal.com to
learn how to accomplish your calling with excellence. Learn to do everything
yourself, or hire trusted Christian Experts from our Marketplace to help.

CONTENTS

INTRODUCTION

Here is a book on health, wealth, and wisdom. This subject will be greeted with mixed response. Doubtless, there will be those who hope it holds the key to Fort Knox and the Fountain of Youth rolled into one. I am sorry, but it doesn't!

There are others who may sneer, "Here comes another of the false *profits*. It's the health and wealth gospel of cash, Cadillacs, and comfort. He is going to tell us how to be a Christian with no sorrow or sickness in sight."

No, that is not the theme of this book. Anyone who can read the Bible ought to know that the demands of discipleship and the cost of commitment are clearly delineated. There is no cheap, easy, or lazy way to serve the Lord Jesus.

If indeed it is to be "all honey and no bees," as some of the "joy boys" teach on television, why did the apostle Paul say this?

> Are they ministers of Christ?—I speak as a fool—I am more: in labors more abundant, in stripes above measure, in prisons more frequently, in deaths often. From the Jews five times I received forty stripes minus one. Three times I was beaten with rods; once I was stoned; three times I was shipwrecked; a night and a day I have been in the deep; in journeys often, in perils of waters, in perils of robbers, in perils of my own countrymen, in perils of the Gentiles, in perils in the city, in perils in the wilderness, in perils in the sea, in perils among false brethren; in weariness and toil, in sleeplessness often, in hunger and thirst, in fastings often, in cold and nakedness—besides the other things, what comes upon me daily: my deep concern for all the churches. (2 Corinthians 11:23-28)

If God wants everybody well, pray tell me, why did the apostle Paul, who had the apostolic gift of healing, leave Trophimus sick at Miletus, or have a thorn in the flesh himself? (See 2 Timothy 4:20; 2 Corinthians 12:7.)

Yet, having given these disclaimers about what this book will not offer you, let me urge you not to miss some of the most exciting and helpful principles in the Word of God, especially in the book of Proverbs.

These studies center primarily in the book of Proverbs, and the Proverbs indeed deal with health, wealth, and wisdom. There is no doubt about it. For example, look at some verses from Proverbs 3:

Health

Do not be wise in your own eyes; fear the LORD and depart from evil. It will be health to your flesh, and strength to your bones. (vv. 7-8)

Wealth

Honor the LORD with your possessions, and with the firstfruits of all your increase; so your barns will be filled with plenty, and your vats will overflow with new wine. (vv. 9-10)

Wisdom

My son, do not despise the chastening of the LORD, nor detest His correction; for whom the LORD loves He corrects, just as a father the son in whom he delights. (vv. 11-12)

The whole thing is brought into a clearer perspective and balance when we learn first of all what a proverb is. A proverb may be defined as a short sentence based on long experience. That is true with human proverbs and also with God's proverbs. But God's proverbs have the added dimension of divine inspiration.

So, these proverbs are gems of wisdom that are principles meant to be God's guide to living. Remember that they are just that—principles and guides. They are not meant to overrule any special plan that God may have for His saints. They are not meant to be ironclad contracts, but principles and guides.

For the Gospel's sake, we may suffer need and rejection, as I have already indicated. Having said that, let me also say that no Christian ought to suffer or fail unless he has ignored God's principles of health, wealth, and wisdom.

One more word is also needed. We need especially to consider what real health, wealth, and wisdom are. For example, Proverbs teaches this truth: not all that the world considers wealth really is. "There is one who makes himself rich, yet has nothing; and one who makes himself poor, yet has great riches" (Proverbs 13:7).

This verse clearly teaches that what the world calls a rich man may indeed not be one. Let me say parenthetically that the unmarried woman reading this should remember what one wise man said: "It is better to marry a man worth a million who doesn't have a cent, than to marry a man who has a million who isn't worth a cent!"

When, therefore, could a rich man in the eyes of the world really be a poor man?

A rich man is a poor man when he seeks satisfaction in his money.

Well did Solomon say, "He who loves silver will not be satisfied with silver..." (Ecclesiastes 5:10a). A man of modest means once commented to a wealthy business tycoon, "I am richer than you are because I have all the money I want and you don't." In fact, not to want something is even better than owning it.

A rich man is a poor man when his wealth increases his worries.

"In the house of the righteous is much treasure: but in the revenues of the wicked is trouble" (Proverbs 15:6).

It is clear that when supposed wealth becomes a burden rather than a blessing, it is not truly wealth. I heard of a man who was sitting on a train near a woman wearing a fantastically large diamond.

He asked the woman, "Pardon me, Madam. I don't mean to be unduly rude or inquisitive, but that is a magnificent gem. Is it perhaps a famous diamond like the Hope Diamond?"

She replied, "No, it is not a well-known diamond like the Hope Diamond. It is the Klopman Diamond, but like the Hope Diamond, it comes with a curse for the person who wears it."

"What kind of a curse?"

The woman answered, "Mr. Klopman!"

The rich man is poor when he becomes a slave to his money.

"Do not overwork to be rich; because of your own understanding, cease!" (Proverbs 23:4). "A faithful man will abound with blessings, but he who hastens to be rich will not go unpunished" (Proverbs 28:20).

Money is a wonderful servant but a poor master. It is bad advice to say "Make all the money you can just so you make it honestly". No one has the right to make all the money he or she can. If he does, he will become a slave to his money. He will be making money when he ought to be doing something else. The man who has no time to play, laugh, love, serve, or worship God is not a rich man, no matter how much money he has.

The rich man is poor when he has no treasure in heaven.

"Will you set your eyes on that which is not? For riches certainly make themselves wings; they fly away like an eagle toward heaven" (Proverbs 23:5). If you want to know how rich you really are, add up all you have that money cannot buy, that death cannot take away. Some wag has quipped, "Money talks. It says good-bye." This is quite true. If it doesn't say good-bye to us, one of these days we will say good-bye to it. Wealth that can be ultimately lost is not true wealth.

The rich man is poor if he dies a Christ-less death.

"Riches do not profit in the day of wrath, but righteousness delivers from death" (Proverbs 11:4).

How poor the supposedly wealthy man will be at the judgment if he does not know Christ. His riches may have "fixed" a traffic ticket for him while he was on earth, but he will not bribe Heaven's Judge. Jesus pulled back the curtain of eternity and gave us a glimpse of one such "rich poor man." "...The rich man also died and was buried. And being in torments..." (Luke 16:22b-23a). It is obvious that his storehouse of treasure had become a storehouse of torment.

What we have seen about true wealth could also be said about health and wisdom. We must be certain to get "the real thing." But remember that God loves you. He takes pleasure in the prosperity of His servants. He really does.

CHAPTER ONE

GOD'S WAY TO WISDOM

The proverbs of Solomon the son of David, king of Israel: to know wisdom and instruction, to perceive the words of understanding, to receive the instruction of wisdom, justice, judgment, and equity; to give prudence to the simple, to the young man knowledge and discretion—a wise man will hear and increase learning, and a man of understanding will attain wise counsel, to understand a proverb and an enigma, the words of the wise and their riddles. The fear of the LORD is the beginning of knowledge, but fools despise wisdom and instruction. (Proverbs 1:1-7)

C an you imagine Almighty God appearing before you and asking, "Is there anything in the world you would like for Me to do for you? What do you want? It is yours for the asking"? For what would you ask Him? A hungry person might request food. An impoverished man might ask for wealth. An egomaniac might desire fame and power.

God did ask someone that question—King Solomon. "On that night God appeared to Solomon, and said to him, 'Ask! What shall I give you?'" (2 Chronicles 1:7).

What an unparalleled opportunity! God laid it all out and instructed, "Solomon, take your pick. Whatever you want is yours for the asking."

What did Solomon request? Fame? Fortune? Power? Pleasure? Women? No, even all of those later became his—and often to his embarrassment and shame.

He made a seemingly unspectacular request: "Now give me wisdom and knowledge, that I may go out and come in before this people; for who can judge this great people of Yours?" (2 Chronicles 1:10). And God answered,

> Then God said to Solomon: "Because this was in your heart, and you have not asked riches or wealth or honor or the life of your enemies, nor have you asked long life—but have asked wisdom and knowledge for yourself, that you may judge My people over whom I have made you king— wisdom and knowledge are granted to you; and I will give you riches and wealth and honor, such as none of the kings have had who were before you, nor shall any after you have the like. (2 Chronicles 1:11-12)

Solomon asked for the right gift in the right manner. And the Book of Proverbs contains a collection of the wisdom God granted King Solomon three millennia ago.

A person may have every earned degree and course of study in every educational institution and still not possess wisdom. Wisdom is the capacity to assimilate and appropriate learning prudently. In the truest sense there is no genuine wisdom apart from God, because wisdom is seeing life from God's point of view.

THE INCOMPARABLE WORTH OF WISDOM

> For wisdom is better than rubies, and all the things one may desire cannot be compared with her. (Proverbs 8:11)

John W. Drakeford has written about "The Five Faces of Wisdom" (*Wisdom for Today's Family*), which are self-discipline (Proverbs 1:2a), understanding (1:2b), wise relationships (1:3a), planning (1:4b), and learning (1:5). God-based wisdom involves all of those and more.

No wonder God was pleased with Solomon's choice! Yet, what makes wisdom so priceless and desirable?

Wisdom Is the Purpose of the Father

Every father worth his salt desires wisdom for his sons and daughters. Solomon was no exception, as we recognize this passage of Scripture is from the king to his son. "My son, if you receive my words, and treasure my commands within you" (Proverbs 2:1). He wants his son to prosper, succeed, and find fulfillment, so he counsels, "Son, if you will only listen to your dad, I will show you how."

These are still words for sons and daughters of the King. If you are a Christian, a child of the King, you believe this counsel is not merely the words of Solomon, but the words of God speaking His wisdom through Solomon. They are not only to Solomon's sons but to God's sons. They are wise words to the "King's kids."

Thus God has distilled this wisdom for us and graciously invites: "Come get it. Here it is. It is yours for the asking." What a picture of His amazing grace!

Wisdom Is the Product of the Spirit

"To know wisdom and instruction, to perceive the words of understanding, to receive the instruction of wisdom..." (Proverbs 1:2-3a). That is, there is to be a teacher. In the case of true wisdom, that instructor is the Holy Spirit of God, Whom the Bible calls "the Spirit of wisdom."

Genuine wisdom is supernatural. So it is exceedingly important to understand the difference between wisdom and common sense, between wisdom and mere knowledge.

Common sense is natural. Some sage remarked, "Common sense is what keeps a horse from betting on a track meet." But most everyone knows that is not even common sense—that's just horse sense. But wisdom is neither. Wisdom is *uncommon* sense. It originated with God, resides in God, emanates from God, and is given as a gift from God.

The difference between wisdom and knowledge is this:

- Knowledge is needed to pass the test in school, but wisdom is needed to pass the test in life.
- Knowledge is learned; wisdom is given.
- Knowledge comes by looking *around*; wisdom comes by looking *up*.

- Knowledge comes by study; wisdom comes by meditation with God.
- Wisdom teaches one how to apply his knowledge.

But wisdom is not a substitute for knowledge, and knowledge is never a stand-in for wisdom. The Bible indicates that a wise person will study. Not long ago a young man requested, "Pray for me. I'm having exams." I am not sure what his request meant. If he meant for me to pray that he would somehow know facts he had not studied, I certainly could not conscientiously pray that God would honor his laziness. No, what I prayed for was that God would give him the wisdom to study. Paul wrote, "Be diligent to present yourself approved to God, a worker who does not need to be ashamed" (2 Timothy 2:15a).

Wisdom is not synonymous with knowledge. Rather, it is the product of the Spirit. Some things in life cannot be learned—those must be given.

Once there was a wealthy gold miner who had an intelligent son destined to take over the business and inherit the father's fortune. The father sent his son back East to study in the finest engineering school and to learn all he could about managing the mines.

The young man studied hard and proudly received his degree and diploma. Returning to the mines he reported to his father, "Dad, I'm ready to go to work. Give me your best mine, and I'll show you how to run it."

The father replied, "No, Son, first you must change into your work clothes and go down into the mine. There you will gain experience. You may start at the bottom and work your way up." But the son insisted, "Look, Father, I've been to school. I've received my diploma. I know more about mining than you will ever know, all due respects. And if you will just give me your best mine I will prove it to you."

And so the father, against his better judgment, gave his son the most productive mine. For a while it did well. Then one day the father received a letter, stating, "Dad, you know that the mine I am working is backed up to the lake. Well, the water is seeping in. We've shored it up, but the shoring does not seem to hold. What do you think we ought to do?" The father did not answer.

In a few more weeks the son wrote again. "Look, Dad, this is serious. We are not able to stop the water. What do you think we ought to do?" Still no answer from the father.

Finally the son frantically wired his father: "IF YOU DO NOT GIVE ME AN ANSWER SOON, WE ARE GOING TO LOSE THE ENTIRE MINE. WHAT SHOULD I DO?" The father wired back: "SHOVE YOUR DIPLOMA IN THAT HOLE."

I would never minimize a proper formal education, but there are certain matters no school can teach you. And in a *greater* sense there are issues about life that can only be learned from God.

Wisdom Is the Presence of the Savior

To know wisdom... (Proverbs 1:2a)

To know wisdom is to know Jesus Christ. If you do not have Jesus, you cannot have wisdom. Paul well expressed this inescapable truth: "But to those who are called, both Jews and Greeks, Christ the power of God and the wisdom of God" (1 Corinthians 1:24). Christ is *the wisdom of God.* This was the idea John the apostle conveyed when he wrote his Gospel:

> In the beginning was the Word, and the Word was with God, and the Word was God... And the Word became flesh and dwelt among us, and we beheld His glory, the glory as of the only begotten of the Father, full of grace and truth. (John 1:1, 14)

The Greek word translated "Word" was *logos. Logos* meant a thought or a concept or the expression or utterance of that thought. Jesus, the living Word, is God and is therefore the perfect expression and extension of the divine wisdom. Real wisdom is discovered only in a personal relationship with Jesus Christ—the wisdom of God, the Word of God, God Himself.

Perhaps there has never been another mind exactly like that of Albert Einstein. But that remarkable genius confessed, "I feel like a man chained. If I could only be freed from the shackles of my intellectual smallness, then I could understand the universe in which I live." Einstein, who propounded the theory of relativity, was overawed when he considered the vastness of the universe he studied. We can only hope he came to know the One Who made it.

The Bible notes that the great are not necessarily the wise. "For the message of the cross is foolishness to those who are perishing..." (1 Corinthians 1:18a). "For since, in the wisdom of God, the world through wisdom did not know God, it pleased God through the foolishness of the message preached to save those who believe" (1 Corinthians 1:21).

God is so wise He cannot let you figure Himself out. He is so good you will never be able to know Him by human wisdom, human perception, or human understanding. No one has a head start on God. All of the philosophers, theologians, and scientists of history could never discover Him through human wisdom.

> For since, in the wisdom of God, the world through wisdom did not know God, it pleased God through the foolishness of the message preached to save those who believe. For Jews request a sign, and Greeks seek after wisdom; but we preach Christ crucified, to the Jews a stumbling block and to the Greeks foolishness, but to those who are called, both Jews and Greeks, Christ the power of God and the wisdom of God. (1 Corinthians 1:21-24)

Yes, one can never know the wisdom of God until Christ, the living wisdom of God, is in his heart. Even the Old Testament saints were wise only because the Spirit of the Lord Jesus dwelt in them. Jesus pointed out, "Your father Abraham rejoiced to see My day, and he saw it and was glad" (John 8:56).

Apart from Christ there is no wisdom. He is made unto us wisdom and righteousness and sanctification and redemption.

Wisdom commences at conversion, but it deepens by discipleship. "The fear of the LORD is the *beginning* of wisdom" (Psalm 111:10a, italics mine). The moment a person is converted to Christ, the wisdom of God comes into him, and the indwelling Spirit of God begins to teach him the truths of the Lord. No wonder wisdom is of such infinite worth.

THE INFALLIBLE WAY TO WISDOM

> My son, if you receive my words, and treasure my commands within you, so that you incline your ear to wisdom, and apply your heart to understanding; yes, if you cry out for discernment, and lift up your voice for understanding, if you seek her as silver, and search for her as for hidden treasures; then you will understand the fear of the LORD, and find the

knowledge of God. For the LORD gives wisdom; from His mouth come knowledge and understanding; He stores up sound wisdom for the upright; He is a shield to those who walk uprightly. (Proverbs 2:1-7)

It is impossible to have knowledge and wisdom apart from Jesus Christ, the living Word, and the Bible, the written Word. First let us think about:

The Pursuit of the Scriptures

You must appreciate the Word of God.
"My son, if you receive My words..." (Proverbs 2:1a). The word "receive" in this verse means to *welcome*. Make yourself a one-person welcoming committee for the Word of God. Do you really appreciate the Word of God?

John Greenleaf Whittier penned these lines:

We search the world for truth.
We cull the good, the true, the beautiful,
From graven stone and written scroll,
And all old flower-fields of the soul;
And, weary seekers of the best,
We come back laden from our quest,
To find that all the sages said
Is in the Book our mothers read.

You must appropriate the Word of God.
"And treasure My commandments within you" (Proverbs 2:1b). Solomon's father, David, wrote: "Your word I have hidden in my heart, that I might not sin against You." (Psalm 119:11). This is even more than welcoming the Word. This is inviting it in and making it feel at home. God's Word must go down deep. It must be hidden in your heart.

Are you hiding it in your heart? Do you saturate your heart, mind, soul, and spirit with it? Are you memorizing it? Are you meditating on it?

The facts of the Bible are not enough. Even the devil knows facts about the Bible. He can quote Scripture. But you must welcome the truths of the Word, appropriate them, and apply them.

You must assimilate the Word of God.

"So that you incline your ear to wisdom..." (Proverbs 2:2a). The Hebrew word for "incline" contains the idea of sharpening and finely tuning the hearing. We are capable of tuning in to whatever we really desire to hear.

We are living in an audiovisual age. Television, radio, CDs and DVDs, and all sorts of derivations abound. All around us people are wearing headsets, in a sense tuning in to what they want to hear but also tuning out what they do not want to hear.

A while back an investment firm had a commercial: "When E. F. Hutton talks, people listen." If only people had this respect and reverence for God and His Word! That is the kind of ear we ought to have for the matchless Word of the living God. If you do not listen, if you do not incline your ear, you might miss something! It has been said that God will not only hold us accountable for what we hear but also for what we would have heard if we had listened.

You must activate the Word of God.

"And apply your heart to understanding" (Proverbs 2:2b). James admonished, "But be doers of the word, and not hearers only, deceiving yourselves" (James 1:22). Activating the Word of God comes by putting it into practice.

Multitudes of Christians sit around admiring the Bible, praising its truths, saying "It's wonderful. It's marvelous." And admire it they should and praise it they should—and it is wonderful and marvelous. But to do nothing about the Word is a sin of dreadful dimensions. It simply is not enough to give lip service to the Word.

Study of the Bible gives you knowledge about God. It is obeying the Bible that gives knowledge of God. But when you translate your theology into shoe leather, you begin to know God deeply. Jesus emphasized this distinction:

> He who has My commandments and keeps them, it is he who loves Me. And he who loves Me will be loved by My Father, and I will love him and manifest Myself to him. (John 14:21)

The next necessity for knowing wisdom is...

The Prayer of the Saints

Yes, if you cry out for discernment, *and* lift up your voice for understanding. (Proverbs 2:3)

You are to pray with intensity.

If you were lost on an expedition or hunting trip—or even on vacation—and you thought someone was within the sound of your voice, you would shout out, "Help me! Show me the way. I'm lost!" Those who have never received Christ are spiritually lost, and they must cry out to Him before they can be rescued and found. And as believers we are still to call out for direction and guidance. God forbid our hurried, half-hearted, lackadaisical, "now-I-lay-me-down-to-sleep" type of prayers. God help us as we often crawl into bed and wave "night-night" to Jesus.

God means business with those who mean business with Him in return. We must become completely serious about wanting Him to lead us. We sing, "Where He leads me I will follow." Do we mean it from the heart, or are we afraid He will do exactly that—He will lead us and we will follow? It could mean a radically different direction in life—soul-winning, surrendering to preach or the mission field, going to the ghetto or slums to minister. If you please, it is risky to pray for His guidance if we are not willing to accept it wholeheartedly.

Solomon often referred to wisdom as a woman, using such pronouns as she and her. "If you seek her as silver, and search for her as for hidden treasures" (Proverbs 2:4). Suppose you heard that the property you own contains the most valuable hidden treasure in the world. Would you look for it? Surely you would. Yet in Christ we have all the riches and treasures of heaven at our disposal. As the old song goes, "I have riches of value untold. Oh, the depth of the riches of love in Christ Jesus."

How tragic that we are not willing to pray with intensity for God to move through us and use us to His glory and honor!

You are to pray with persistency.

What a difference it would make if all of us Christians would seek wisdom as we do wealth! Many believers are involved in all kinds of moneymaking schemes, some solid and others suspect. I am sure many professing Christians across our country may play the lottery in the hopes of "striking it rich" at the expense of thousands or even millions of others who have never won. Gambling in any form is an outright sin, but let me emphasize this: failing to seek God's wisdom is a sin much greater.

Many were shocked when Alex Rodriguez signed a $252 million dollar 10-year contract to play professional baseball. Think with me for a minute. Do you pursue God's knowledge and wisdom like an athlete pursues excellence on the athletic field? Do you? Paul spoke of the Greco-Roman athletes of his day: "Now they do it to obtain a perishable crown, but we for an imperishable crown" (1 Corinthians 9:25b).

We are to pray with insistence and importunity, even as the friend who knocked at midnight wanting to borrow three loaves of bread (see Luke 11:5ff). We are to "wrestle" with the Lord, as did Jacob with the angel at the Brook Jabbok (see Genesis 32:24ff). We are to cry with Jacob, "I will not let You go unless You bless me!" We are to ask, knock, and seek.

You are to pray with expectancy.

"Then you will understand the fear of the LORD, and find the knowledge of God. For the LORD gives wisdom; from His mouth *come* knowledge and understanding" (Proverbs 2:5-6).

If you pray believing and under the blood of Christ, the Lord will give you wisdom. Sometimes when we pray we are not certain of the will of God. And the Bible declares, "Now this is the confidence that we have in Him, that if we ask anything according to His will, He hears us" (1 John 5:14). Nail that down. We can pray with confidence in Him. If we do, we can ask whatever He places on our hearts, and He will hear us. No ifs, ands, or buts.

If we have learned nothing else in this study, it is: God wills for us to have wisdom. James 1:5-7 explains it:

> If any of you lacks wisdom, let him ask of God, who gives to all liberally and without reproach, and it will be given to him. But let him ask in faith, with no doubting, for he who doubts is like a wave of the sea driven and tossed by the wind. For let not that man suppose that he will receive anything from the Lord.

So when you ask with persistence, and you make your petition with fervor, then you can wait with expectancy. The phrase "without reproach" means that God will not scold you for asking. He is never going to retort, "Why are you bothering Me again? Are you wanting more wisdom?" No—to quote the poet "out of His infinite wisdom He giveth and giveth and giveth again" (Annie Johnson Flint, "He Giveth More Grace").

Thou art coming to a King
Large petitions with You bring

For His grace and power are such
None can ever ask too much.
—John Newton

The Presence of the Savior

This carries us right back to where we started. You cannot avoid it; cannot go around it, over it, or under it. You cannot tunnel underneath it. There is no way to wisdom outside of Jesus Christ.

> For the LORD gives wisdom; from His mouth come knowledge and understanding; He stores up sound wisdom for the upright; He is a shield to those who walk uprightly; He guards the paths of justice, and preserves the way of His saints. (Proverbs 2:6-8)

This is a promise for the saints, those who are saved. In the Lord Jesus Christ there is security and soundness. In Him there is salvation, for our Lord is a buckler and shield. He preserves the way of the saints, those who belong to Him.

Christ is made unto us wisdom. He is the Way. When you repent of your sin and receive Him as your Lord and Savior, you will possess this marvelous gift that Solomon wanted more than all else—wisdom.

Without this God-granted wisdom, life is a walking death, a journey through a labyrinth of confusion and fear.

But in Christ we have the Way, the Truth, and the Life. As the song describes Him, "He's everything to me." To have Jesus Christ as your Savior is to embrace all the wisdom of God Himself.

CHAPTER TWO

REMOVING ROADBLOCKS TO PROSPERITY

He that covers his sins will not prosper: but whoever confesses and forsakes them shall have mercy. (Proverbs 28:13)

This entire book is devoted to discovering that *God's wisdom is better than gold*. Some may read a few lines and lay it aside, commenting, "Hmmppff, that's just more preacher talk." Others will continue to read with misgivings but perhaps with no intention of adhering to the principles.

But maybe this is where you come in. You truly want to know God's wisdom. William H. Cook, in his classic *Success, Motivation, and the Scriptures,* said:

> A right definition of success is important from two sides—from the side of having God in it, and from the side of having achievement in it. Defining success without having God in the definition leaves man without the blessing of God upon his life. Yet having God in the life and still not achieving is adding insult to the Infinite.

God knows
> More about success [or prosperity] than man does
> More about man's needs than man does
> More about goal-setting than man does
> More about inner confidence than man does
> More about power than man does, and
> More about planning life than man does.

"Since God knows all those things and provides the very route to our success, isn't it incredible that we would leave Him out of our plans?"

Are you interested in being prosperous, in being successful? I hope you are. God wants you to be prosperous. Are you aware the Bible says, "Let the LORD be magnified, who has pleasure in the prosperity of His servant?" (Psalm 35:27b).

As a matter of fact, one of the most unqualified promises in the Bible is found in Psalm 1. The psalmist compares a righteous man to a tree planted by the rivers of water. He writes concerning that type of person: "And Whatever he does shall prosper" (v. 3c). Whatever he does!

Immediately most people think of prosperity as being rich—owning a mansion, having servants waiting on you hand and foot, possessing a fleet of Rolls-Royces or Mercedes, cornering stocks, bonds, and securities. But God is not guaranteeing material wealth. Many of you became all excited when you read this chapter title because you were thinking, *I'm going to get a lot of money.* In reality, you may have more money right now than God can trust you with!

When I write about prosperity, I am not thinking primarily about money, even though God may allow you to have material wealth. If you think I am, you really do not understand the intent of the Bible or the meaning of the biblical word "prosperity." God wants you prosperous but not necessarily rich.

Prosperity means that you will live a life of general welfare where God meets your needs and you enjoy His blessings. That is the Bible's view of prosperity. Are you disappointed? You shouldn't be.

And God's plan for prosperity is found in Proverbs 28:13: "He that covers his sins will not prosper..." The major reason we do not prosper in God's sight is rather simple. There is unconfessed sin in our hearts. It is that plain. I could as easily turn it around and let it read like this: "He that uncovers his sin will prosper."

There is an adage, "To err is human; to forgive, divine." That is true. But we could also express it, "To err is human, and to try to cover it up is also human."

One wise observer has remarked, "He who falls into sin is a human. He who grieves over his sin is a saint. He who boasts of his sin is a devil." If you are a saint you may sin. But if you are a saint, you will grieve over that sin and will want to do something about it. So this verse is for you. "He that covers his sins will not prosper: but whoever confesses and forsakes them will have mercy."

Rene Pascal struck home when he wrote: "There are only two kinds of men: the righteous who believe themselves sinners; the rest, sinners, who believe themselves righteous."

Think with me for a moment about some factors that will help to remove the obstacle of sin on the pathway to prosperity. The first is:

THE COSTS OF COVERED SIN

"He that covers his sins will not prosper." This is only half a sentence in Proverbs, but this principle is substantiated throughout the Word of God. The particular passage I have selected is Psalm 51, one of David's "penitential psalms."

Psalm 51 is an outpouring of his heart following his sins of lust, adultery, murder, cheating, lying, and more. David was called "a man after God's own heart." Today we would call him a Christian, a believer, a saint. I confidently expect to meet David in heaven— David the sweet singer of Israel but also David the severe sinner who begged for forgiveness and mercy.

David committed the sin of adultery with Bathsheba, the wife of Uriah the Hittite. Then, in an attempt to cover his sin and to have Bathsheba for himself, he ordered Uriah to be exposed to the enemy on the battlefield where he would be slain. He wanted Uriah's death to look like a military action, but it was a murderous atrocity.

You know "the rest of the story," as Paul Harvey would put it. Uriah was put into the heat of battle. The troops withdrew, leaving him vulnerable and he was killed. You cry, "Horrible!" Yes, it was. And yet David was a man who deeply loved God and who tried to cover up his sins. Even though he was a man of God, he paid the price for his sins in trying to gloss them over.

Covered Sin Dirties the Soul

In Psalm 51:1-2 David cried out, "Have mercy upon me, O God, according to Your lovingkindness: according to the multitude of Your tender mercies, blot out my transgressions. Wash me thoroughly from my iniquity and cleanse me from my sin."

David felt dirty—and was dirty. If you are a Christian, then when you sin, you are going to feel filthy within and without. The most miserable person on the face of the earth, I believe, is not a hell-bent sinner but a heaven-bound saint who has fallen into sin. Talk of the blues and the pits. There is no feeling worse than being out of fellowship with one's Savior! Henry Wadsworth Longfellow penned these lines:

> Man-like is it to fall in sin,
> Fiend-like is it to dwell therein,
> Christ-like is it all sin to forsake.

Lady Macbeth of Shakespeare's play lamented, after her collusion in a murder: "All the perfumes of Arabia will not sweeten this little hand." David probably bathed in a marble tub and used perfumed soap. Perhaps he slept on silken sheets. He wore a royal robe. And yet he was a king who felt dirty.

He pled, "Wash me... Cleanse me." Sin defiles and dirties us. If you can sin and not feel dirty, it is because you have never been saved. No hog ever feels dirty. He likes mud and swill. Why? Because that is his nature. A hog doesn't worry about dirt. In fact, he loves it.

One of the basic differences between a child of God and a child of the devil is: When the child of God sins, he feels dirty. An unsaved man leaps into sin and loves it. A saved man lapses into sin and loathes it. You see, sin grieves the blessed Holy Spirit within the life of a believer. If you can sin without feeling dirty and unclean, it is a sign the Holy Spirit does not dwell within you.

Covered Sin Dominates the Mind

In Psalm 51:3, David prayed, "For I acknowledge my transgressions: and my sin is always before me." Night and day, day and night, what David had done reverberated in his consciousness. It etched itself upon his soul. *It dominated his mind.* He could not forget it.

There is yet another means of knowing whether or not you are genuinely saved: *whether you can sin and forget it.* If you can sin and forget, shrug your shoulders and lay it aside, it is proof you have never been born again. God is holy and righteous. He is grieved by sin. Habakkuk declared of God, "You are of purer eyes than to behold evil, and cannot not look on wickedness" (1:13a). And so David confessed, "My sin is always before me."

You say, "You mean I'm going to be thinking consciously about my sin all the time?" No, not necessarily all the time, but you may shove it out of your conscious mind, and it will seep down into your subconsciousness. If you kick your sin out the front door, it will run around the house and come in through the basement window.

It will show up as a migraine headache or as an irritable disposition. It will manifest itself as the inability to concentrate on your work. It will rear its head in your inability to pray effectually and fervently.

"If I regard iniquity in my heart, the Lord will not hear" (Psalm 66:18). It will be seen in a lack of peace with God or with anyone else, certainly including yourself. Your sin will be there like a monkey on your back until it is acknowledged, uncovered, confessed, and forgiven.

There are two kinds of wounds to the human psyche. One is sorrow; the other is guilt. Sorrow is a clean wound. Somehow your heart will heal as the Holy Spirit applies His healing balm. He will pour in "the oil of gladness." Time and the grace of God will heal that broken heart because sorrow is a clean wound.

But guilt is dirty and will never heal, festering and festering, until it is confessed and put away. It must be cleansed by the antiseptic of Calvary before it can be healed. Are you carrying around a load of guilt? Does it dominate your mind?

Shakespeare, a perceptive student of human nature, wrote: "Trust me, no torture the poets can name can match that fierce, unutterable pain he feels, who day and night, devoid of rest, carries his own accuser within his breast."

Covered Sin Depresses the Heart

Psalm 51:8 states, "Make me to hear joy and gladness; that the bones which You have broken may rejoice." Then in verse 12a, he prayed "Restore to me the joy of Your salvation."

The man after God's own heart lost his joy and toppled into a state of depression. If you do not have joy, do you wonder why? The reason is sin. Not two reasons, not three—but one. Sin can remove the joy from your life.

"Wait a minute," you may respond, "Nobody is going to be happy all the time." I never mentioned *happiness*. I am referring to joy. Happiness depends on what happens. Thus, we call it happiness. If your "hap" is good, you are happy. If your hap is bad, you are unhappy.

Joy is a different situation altogether. The Bible commands, "Rejoice in the Lord always" (Philippians 4:4a). The Christian is to "rejoice with joy inexpressible and full of glory" (1 Peter 1:8c). Within your heart as a Christian there is to be a fountain of Spirit-prompted joy. "The fruit of the Spirit is love, joy..." (Galatians 5:22a). Augustine prayed, "There is a joy which is not given to the ungodly, but to those who love You for Thine own sake, whose joy Thou Thyself art. And this is the happy life, to rejoice in You, of You, for You; this it is, and there is no other."

Covered Sin Diseases the Body

Consider verse eight: "Make me to hear joy and gladness; that the bones which You have broken may rejoice" (Psalm 51). David felt broken, crushed, and shattered from his guilt. He was in a veritable pressure cooker. He felt as if he were about to explode or, as one song expresses it, "coming apart at the seams." In Psalm 32:3-4a David testified, "When I kept silent, my bones grew old through my groaning all day long. For day and night Your hand was heavy upon me."

Some people who believe we can lose our salvation think that God simply casts us away when we sin. To the contrary, God does not let us out of His hand, but rather closes His hand all the tighter. And the pressure becomes more and more intense. That is why David burst out, "God, You are crushing the life out of me!"

When we are out of fellowship with God, it seems as though we are being put into a vise and are being crushed, with all of the life being squeezed from our bodies. God is putting on the pressure. He does not discard us. He deals with us lovingly but firmly.

A person cannot live under this pressure for long before it will affect him physically, even though the pressure is psychological. It can lead to "psychosomatic illness," which means a sickness in which the soul (psyche) makes the body (*soma*) sick. If you have not read it, find a copy of the classic *None of These Diseases* by Dr. S. I. McMillen to discover how sin can manifest itself in psychosomatic illnesses.

Sin will disease and dissipate your body. It will do to your body what sand and grit will do to machinery. To have health, begin with rooting out your sin.

The book of Proverbs speaks plenty about how to be healthy physically. One tonic for health is found in 17:22a: "A merry heart does good like medicine." When joy flees, your medicine is sapped. The joy of the Lord is a tonic for the heart, mind, soul, and spirit.

There is a quality about the joy of the Lord which enables you to sleep at night, which aids you in enjoying and digesting your food, which helps you to stand up straight with your organs and bones aligned so you can breathe deeply and maintain your muscle tone, and which makes you want to move out and exercise.

Nehemiah 8:10c affirms: "The joy of the LORD is your strength." The cost of covered sin is the losing of your joy. Without joy you feel crushed and debilitated. Before long your body can become diseased and dissipated. David prayed, "Restore to me the joy of Your salvation" (Psalm 51:12a). The joy can be lost by the believer—not the salvation, but the *joy* of it. The most miserable person on earth is not a lost person, but a saved person out of fellowship with God.

Covered Sin Defiles the Spirit

In Psalm 51:10b David petitioned the Lord, "And renew a steadfast spirit within me." David had a wrong spirit, a defiled spirit. What is that kind of spirit? First, it is a critical spirit. When a person has covered sin in his life, he often tries to uncover the sin in someone else's life. That is a psychological fact. All you have to do is look around you. The person who constantly points the finger at others and sits in judgment of them is wrestling with covered sin in his own heart.

Throughout my ministry I have watched, oftentimes helplessly, as numerous believers pass through various stages of backsliding. Sometimes all I have been able to do is pray for them. What happens is a Christian will become entangled with sin in his life—sometimes a moral sin—at other times a sin of attitude. Perhaps he feels someone has neglected him, abused him, or refused him. And a root of bitterness may sink within the soil of his soul. Regardless of what it is, that Christian will try to cover it up.

He may still attend with regularity at church. He acts as though all is peaches and cream. He smiles and glad-hands. He sings and goes through the motions of praise. But lurking inside there is covered sin. That Christian begins to backslide and finds it easy to become critical of other people.

With a jaundiced eye he begins to look for faults in the church leadership, in the deacons, in the pastor, in the Sunday School teachers, in the various programs of the church. Whether or not he is willing to admit it, he feels that somehow finding fault in others will justify his own sin.

He will become increasingly caustic and may even drop out altogether, and chances are he may not even attend another church, much less move his membership. His excuse will likely be, "Those folks down at the church are nothing but a bunch of hypocrites." But the problem all the time has been his sin which has led to a smokescreen of criticism. Covered sin has defiled him and ruined his effectiveness in God's kingdom.

Let me illustrate. One day his "pastor", Nathan the prophet, came to call on King David. Nathan drew David in with, "King, there is a problem in the kingdom, and you need to judge it." David asked, "What is it?"

"King, in the kingdom there is a very poor man," Nathan replied. "He has nothing he can really claim as his own, except he did have one little ewe lamb that was like a child to him. It was a pet. Why, the ewe stayed in the house with him. He loved that lamb as he would have loved his own child."

Nathan continued, "King, this poor man lived next door to a very rich man. The rich man already had more than his heart could possibly desire. He had flocks of sheep in abundance. He had huge herds of cattle.

Now, when the rich man had a stranger that happened upon him, he went over to the poor man's house, stole the fellow's little ewe lamb, killed it, and barbecued it. Then he fed it to the stranger. What should be done to that rich man, O King?"

David was livid with rage. He clenched his fists, rose up from the throne, and announced, "Surely this man is worthy of death, but he will have to make a four-fold restitution!" David had unknowingly sentenced himself in his own court.

Nathan pointed a bony finger at the king and pronounced, "You are the man" (2 Samuel 12:7a).

What I want you to see is that David was quick to judge the man of Nathan's parable when he had a far worse sin in his own heart. It was serious to steal an animal but far worse to steal a woman, another man's wife. It was severe to kill a pet, but far worse to slay a man.

Here was a man David, with a log in his own eye, thinking about removing a speck from someone else's eye. Here he was covering his own sin but trying to uncover sin in another's life. Sin caused David to have a bitter, censorious spirit. God deliver us from that kind of people.

Covered Sin Destroys the Testimony

In verses 12-15 of Psalm 51, David begged:

Restore to me the joy of Your salvation; and uphold me by Your generous Spirit. Then I will teach transgressors Your ways; and sinners shall be converted to You. Deliver me from the guilt of bloodshed, O God, The God of my salvation: and my tongue shall sing aloud of Your righteousness. O Lord, open my lips: and my mouth shall show forth Your praise.

What happened? Covered sin shut his lips and stopped his mouth. It kept him from witnessing and from singing. Can you imagine the singer of Israel with no song? That was like a mute mockingbird or a throatless thrush. David confessed, "When I get my heart right, then will I teach transgressors Your ways, and sinners will be converted."

Perhaps you are not a soul-winner. Maybe you are. If not one now, maybe you were a soul-winner at one time. One of the chief reasons Christians are not soul-winners is that they have covered sins in their lives. Sin intimidates you, makes you fearful, and causes you to feel inadequate about sharing your testimony.

When many Christians start to witness the devil whispers, "You hypocrite, how dare you witness about the Lord Jesus when there is covered sin in your life. How can you possibly lead another person to Christ? You rotten sinner, you!" Sin seals our lips and destroys our testimony.

Andrew Murray, one of the greatest Christians who ever lived, laid it on the line: "There are two classes of Christians: soul winners and backsliders." Covered sin stifles joy, then the praise withers and dries up, too.

You think all the foregoing is terrible? I have saved the worst fact about covered sin until last.

Covered Sin Dishonors the Lord

David confessed, "Against You, You only, have I sinned" (Psalm 51:4a). What tore up David's heart was that he sinned against God. David did not sin primarily against his own body, not mainly against Bathsheba, not even basically against poor Uriah... or against the Kingdom of Israel... *but against God!*

A sign you are truly saved is when it breaks your heart that you have broken God's heart. You have sinned against Him. The unsaved man merely worries about being caught and frets about the consequences of his sin, but he doesn't care about God's feelings.

However, a true Christian realizes he has not only broken God's law... but also God's heart. David finally uncovered his sin and repented, "O God, I have sinned. I have sinned against You and done this evil in Your sight. My dear Lord, how could I do such a thing?"

What makes me want to deal with my own sin is not primarily my fear of what God might do to me. I love Him. *I am motivated by my fear of what my sin will do against Him.*

If you are not saved this will have absolutely no appeal to you. A slave only fears his master's whip, but a son fears his father's displeasure. "Against You, You only, have I sinned, and done this evil in Your sight." Now, the second factor:

THE CONFESSION OF COMMITTED SIN

He that covers his sins will not prosper: but whoever confesses and forsakes them will have mercy. (Proverbs 28:13)

What is a good confession of sin? Have you ever really thought of that? There is a proper, God-honored way to confess your sin. It is threefold.

Sin Must Be Exposed

Who is going to expose your sin? You cannot do it. You are not qualified to do it. You do not possess the tools with which to expose your sin.

The Bible states that "the heart is deceitful above all things, and desperately wicked: who can know it?" (Jeremiah 17:9). And a wicked heart can never diagnose a wicked heart. And a sinful heart is never going to condemn a sinful heart. There is only One who is going to expose a wicked heart, and He is the Holy Spirit.

Jesus Himself explained, "And when He is come, He [the Holy Spirit] will convict the world of sin" (John 16:8a). It is His work to expose sin in your life. Rather than trying to probe around in your own "innards"— analyzing and psychoanalyzing yourself, dissecting yourself into little pieces and putting yourself back together—you need to allow the Holy Spirit to expose that sin in your life. He alone is capable of doing that.

You need to pray with the psalmist, "Search me, O God, and know my heart: try me, and know my anxieties: And see if there be any wicked way in me, and lead me in the way everlasting" (Psalm 139:23-24).

Whereas the Holy Spirit of God will *expose* sin in your life, the devil will *exploit* sin in your life. What is the difference? When the Holy Spirit exposes sin, the only sin He will expose is sin you have tried to cover by yourself. Catch this now. Sin that you have uncovered, the Holy Spirit covers.

When we cover it, He uncovers it. When we uncover it, He covers it. Strange? No. "He that covers his sins will not prosper." The moment I confess, "Look, Lord, I did it. I confess it. I put it under the blood of Jesus Christ," the Holy Spirit moves into action and covers it with forgiveness.

And when He covers it, it is forgiven and forgotten forever, never to be brought up again. Hebrews 8:12b promises, "Their sins and their iniquities will I remember no more."

But the devil will exploit your sin. When a sin has already been uncovered by you and then covered by the Holy Spirit, the devil will try his hardest to uncover it one more time. The devil, Satan, will try to dredge up forgiven—and should be forgotten—sin to make you feel guilty.

When that sin has been covered with the blood and is forgiven, and then the devil tries to exploit it, to drag it out, recognize his dirty work for what it is. When that sin is forgiven, it can no longer be held to your account. Such guilt over sin which God has covered is not Holy Spirit conviction. Rather, it is satanic accusation.

The devil is attempting to accuse you and thus to defeat your confidence in Christ. Put the devil in his place. Plead the blood of the Lord Jesus: "Devil, my sin is under the blood. You and all your demons can do nothing to parade that sin before me. Get You behind me, Satan!" You no longer need to be haunted by the ghost of guilt. What God has forgiven, let no one exhume from the past.

Martin Luther, the founder of the Protestant Reformation, had a dream, a vision, or a nightmare. He was not sure what it was. But he was awakened in the middle of the night to see standing at the foot of his bed a figure he believed was none other than the devil himself.

The devil had a scroll, and on that scroll were the sins Luther had committed. Luther admitted the list was accurate. The devil was reading them, one sin after another. Pointing a fiery finger into Luther's face. He condemned and accused him, "What hope of heaven do you have?"

At that moment, Luther felt his very soul slipping down into hell. Then the Lord intervened, "Tell the devil to unroll the rest of the scroll." Luther instructed the devil "Unroll the scroll entirely." The devil refused. Luther then commanded, "In the name of Jesus, unroll the scroll." Reluctantly, Satan unrolled it.

There printed across the bottom in crimson ink were these words: "This entire sin account of Martin Luther paid in full by the blood of Jesus Christ!"

The devil does not want you to have the entire scroll.

When the Holy Spirit exposes your sin, He will expose your sin specifically. He will spell out precisely what you thought or felt or spoke or did.

If the devil cannot call forth a sin that has already been covered with the blood of Jesus, he will take a different tack. He will endeavor to make you feel bad all over. You will weakly rely on feelings, and you will often feel lousy. The devil will be general about your sins. In this case he will not accuse with a specific sin, but he will try to make you feel unworthy, of no account, and sinful, even if you have "confessed up."

Do you ever feel unacceptable, unworthy, inadequate? That does not come from God the Holy Spirit. That is not His approach. The Bible says concerning the Holy Spirit, "He made us accepted in the Beloved" (Ephesians 1:6b). He does not make us feel unaccepted once we have accepted Christ. Those feelings of unworthiness are the work of the devil.

When the Spirit exposes sin in your life, He lays bare a specific sin, one which has not yet been dealt with. He will spell it out within your heart: "You lied" or "You were proud" or "You were selfish." Whatever it is, the Holy Spirit will name it. Like the doctor feeling for symptoms, the Spirit will put His finger on the sore spot and push. But the devil will often vaguely accuse you, giving you an overall feeling of unworthiness.

Sin Must Be Expressed

For confession to take place, that sin must be exposed and expressed to the Lord. You must name that sin. You must tell God precisely what you did.

A pernicious problem with many of us—and the reason we seldom have peace within—is that we like to sin retail and confess wholesale. We like to sin all during the day and then before going to sleep, we pray speedily, "Father, forgive all my sins. Amen."

Or we might pray like this: "Father, if I have sinned, forgive me." That will not make it. If the Spirit convicts you specifically, God expects you to confess your sin the same way.

Not only must you *name it*—you must *nail it*. "Lord, I have done this. I have thought that. I have had a bad attitude. I confess all of it." When you tell God about it—the jealousy, the lust, the dishonesty, and bitterness, you name it—then you are about to have victory over it.

Your sin must be exposed. It must be expressed. Away with this situation of sinning retail and confessing wholesale. We have often sung, "Count your many blessings, name them one by one, And it will surprise you what the Lord hath done." I like that. But sometimes I would like to add another verse, "Count your many sins name them one by one, and it will surprise you what you have done." Name those sins before the throne.

Sin Must Be Expelled

Return to the text, "He that covers his sins will not prosper: but whoso confesses and forsakes them will have mercy." It is not enough to confess without forsaking. Here is where many of us fail. The sin is exposed and expressed but is not expelled. And we do not have mercy and do not prosper.

Somehow we have the mistaken notion that we can attend church, shed a few crocodile tears, mumble a formula, pass through the motions, and continue to sin. No wonder our lives are frayed and tattered. Away with our counterfeit, bogus confessions, for God will not honor them in the bank of heaven.

Exposed, expressed in confession, and expelled. Sin must be forsaken. We must write *kaput*, finished, over our sins.

Now, even though Pharaoh was not a believer, he presents an example of an improper confession. In Exodus 9:27, "And Pharaoh sent and called for Moses and Aaron, and said unto them, 'I have sinned this time. The LORD is righteous, and my people and I are wicked.'"

My, that sounds like a good confession, does it not? Yet his was a dishonest confession. This seemingly potent confession came on the heels of what is recorded in Exodus 9 beginning in verse 22. In answer to God's command, Moses "stretched out your hand toward heaven… and the LORD sent thunder and hail… so there was hail, and fire mingled with the hail" (23-24).

When God unleashed all of the elements of heaven and rained down fire mixed with hail, thunder, and lighting, Pharaoh begged for mercy.

But when the storm abated, the lightning stopped, the thunder ceased, and the hail and fire were gone, so was his so-called repentance. Look at Exodus 9:34: "And when Pharaoh saw that the rain, the hail, and the thunder had ceased, he sinned yet more, and he hardened his heart, he and his servants."

Even though Pharaoh was not a believer, a certain principle is the same. In the life of a Christian, sin which is not expelled hardens the believer's heart. Christian, unless sin is confessed properly, you are not going to prosper.

How many times have you promised God, "O God, forgive me. Cleanse me, and I'll do what you want"? Perhaps your baby or another loved one was desperately ill, and you begged for your flesh and blood to be spared. Your prayer was answered, but how quickly you forgot your half-hearted promise! Recall when you sorely needed that job, you were in dread difficulty, you were up the creek and about to capsize.

Yet, the repentance born in the storm died in the calm. And as soon as the fire, the hail, the thunder, the lightning, and the storm were removed, you sinned all the more.

What must happen to the sin in your life? Exposed. Expressed in confession. And expelled. "He that covers his sins will not prosper: but whoso confesses and forsakes them will have mercy."

Do you want prosperity? There is the clear-cut answer. *Face the cost of covered sin,* then make *the confession of committed sin, and know the joy of forgiven sin.*

The way to prosperity is to hate sin in your life and in the lives of others; to eschew sin; to flee sin; to expose sin; to confess sin; to expel sin.

John Newton, a "wild man" tamed by Jesus Christ, wrote:

> Thus, while His death my sin displays
>   In all its blackest hue,
> Such is the mystery of grace,
>   It seals my pardon too.
> With pleasing grief, and mournful joy,
>   My spirit now is fill'd,
> That I should such a life destroy,—
>   Yet live by Him I kill'd!

CHAPTER THREE

HOW NOT TO RAISE A FOOL

How long, you simple ones, will you love simplicity? For scoffers delight in their scorning, and fools hate knowledge. Turn at My rebuke; surely I will pour out My Spirit on you; I will make My words known to you. (Proverbs 1:22-23)

T he word "fool" is despised. It grates on the nerves. And you are thinking, *Doesn't the Bible say we aren't to call anyone a fool?* I make it a point never to call a person that; it is not my prerogative. But God is God, and He has every right to designate anyone a fool.

The psalmist observes: "The fool has said in his heart, There is no God" (Psalm 14:1a). God called the rich farmer a fool: "Fool! This night your soul will be required of you" (Luke 12:20a).

"Fool" in these passages and throughout Proverbs means a spiritually insensitive clod who lives for himself apart from the control of God's Spirit. God has aptly described the fool in the pages of His Word. He also traces the development of the fool, the person who is bent on "kicking over the traces" and living as though there is no God and no eternity.

No one is born a fool. Fools are self-made, generally with a bit of help from their parents and associates. Proverbs 22:15a appropriately teaches, "Foolishness is bound up in the heart of a child." That is, the seeds of foolishness are there, but people generally water those seeds.

Fool in the Bible does not refer to a person who is mentally deficient. A retarded person is not a fool. As a matter of fact, the Word speaks gently and sweetly concerning the emotionally and mentally handicapped, teaching us to love and to nurture them. In the Bible a fool is the person who is morally and spiritually deficient. The problem is not with the head—but the heart. And the fool is a fool by choice.

Far too many parents are inculcating foolishness into the hearts and minds of their own children. Let's give some of the parents the benefit of the doubt. Many of them are doing it unwittingly. I want to teach you how not to raise a fool.

Proverbs 1:22 presents us the formula for the making of a fool. There are three recognizable steps a person passes through in order to become a fool. "How long, you simple ones, will you love simplicity?"

A person begins life as what the Bible calls a simple one. Simple one does not imply a "simpleton." Neither does it indicate a person without good sense, but rather an open-minded "happy-go-lucky" person.

But then a person moves from simplicity to scornfulness. "For scorners delight in their scorning." Step two: he becomes a scorner.

Then there is step three: "And fools hate knowledge..." There you have it. He is simple at first. Next, he is a scorner. And finally he becomes an outright fool.

THE IGNORANCE OF THE SIMPLE

I want to call him an ignorant person—not one who does not have intelligence. You can have a certain amount of intelligence and still be ignorant. Never equate knowledge with intelligence. So notice what we will call the ignorance of the simple. What makes a simple person?

He Loves Simplicity

Notice 1:22: "How long, you simple ones, will you love simplicity?" He likes his lifestyle. It's easy, happy, carefree. And he delights in it. He has virtually no responsibilities and problems. He follows the line of least resistance. You cannot pin him down to the deeper verities of life.

You have heard of the Greek orator Demosthenes. At first he was not articulate. So, he put pebbles in his mouth and argued with the ocean waves until he learned to make his voice heard.

One day he was speaking to a huge throng about the vital matters of life, death, and eternity. They were not paying attention; their minds were gathering wool.

He discerned their inattention and announced, "Ladies and gentlemen, I want to tell you a story. Once there was a man who had a heavy load of sticks on his back. He had to cross a mountain in spite of being tired and weary.

"Another man came alongside of him. He was leading a donkey and asked, 'Why do you carry those sticks on your back? Why not rent my donkey and let the donkey carry the sticks over the mountain?' They haggled about price, and then the man rented the donkey. And the man who rented the donkey and the owner started over the mountain.

"The sun became scorching hot. The renter stopped to rest for a while. He tied the donkey and sat down in the shade of the donkey's body. The owner of the donkey also sat down, but there was not enough shade for the two of them."

"The owner said, 'I'm sorry, but you'll have to move.' 'I will not move!' was the angry reply, 'This is my spot,' retorted the renter.

"'No, it is my spot. The donkey belongs to me, and so does the shade,' insisted the owner. The answer came back, 'I know the donkey belongs to you, but since I rented the donkey, the shade of the donkey belongs to me.' The owner angrily made his point, 'I merely rented you the donkey. I didn't rent you the shade of the donkey.' And they became involved in a furious argument."

Demosthenes described the argument and then walked off the stage. After a while the people yelled and clamored for him to return. Finally, he came back. The crowd asked, "What happened? Who won the argument? To whom did the shade belong? To the man who rented the donkey or the one who owned it?"

Demosthenes replied: "I have been talking to you about the issues of life and death, and you were not concerned. Now you clamor to know who owns the shade of a donkey!"

There is a prime example of simple-minded people. They love "baubles, bangles, and beads." "When is my next cigarette, my next can of beer, my next cable TV show, my next soap opera?" they ask. They do not want to hear God's Word. And even if they are present in a service, they do not want to listen.

The simple will complain about a sermon being too long but they will sit for hours and watch TV until their eyes become big as coconuts and their brains the size of a pea.

He Lacks Understanding

Proverbs 9:4 continues to describe the simple one. "Whosoever is simple, let him turn in here: as for him that lacks understanding..." If a person loves simplicity, he is going to lack understanding. Neither will he know the truths of God's Word.

I repeat: one can be intelligent and still lack moral and spiritual understanding. Will Rogers, the late humorist, opined: "Everybody is ignorant, just on different subjects."

The first mark of a simple man is that he loves simplicity. The second earmark is: he lacks understanding. The third is:

He Is Easily Led

"The simple believes every word, but the prudent man considers well his steps" (Proverbs 14:15).

In the Hebrew "simple" means open. When you come down to it, it carries the idea of "gullible." The simple man will believe most anything. You can buy the Brooklyn Bridge. Yeah. You can make a killing in horse races. Yeah. You can do whatever you want and live however you please. It sounds great, and the simple love it.

There is the sequence. Loves simplicity. Lacks understanding. And then he is easily led. Nature abhors a vacuum. Since everybody believes something, if one doesn't believe what is right, he will believe what is wrong. The gullible person is a sitting duck; Madison Avenue has him like putty in its hands. False religions, rock music, lewd entertainment, sinful friends—all of these lead the simple around like a bull with a ring in his nose.

Have you noticed the tabloid papers, and even rather reputable newspapers, and their lists of what's "in" and what's "out?" That is absolutely ridiculous. Yet the religion of the simple is the "cult of conformity." It should make no difference what some movie star or rock idol wears or doesn't wear. Jesus will always be "in." The simple-minded person will always be "out" no matter how he tries to conform and follow every new fad that comes down the road.

Many people have simple children. Not stupid—but simple. They love simplicity. They are flippant about the truths of God. They lack understanding, and when they arrive at junior high school and senior high they are going to be led astray and drawn in. "Man, come on, try this weed. Take this pill. Sniff this stuff. Hey, everybody's doing it!" The open mind and plastic convictions of the simple teenager make him vulnerable.

He Is Liable For Judgment

"A prudent man," says the Word, "foresees evil and hides himself, but the simple pass on and are punished" (Proverbs 22:3).

A simple-minded youngster, or adult for that matter, is oblivious to danger. That is often why a simple-minded kid will continue to total your automobiles, amass a raft of traffic tickets, and disobey the speed and safety laws. He barges through life as though he is the only person. And if he prepares for his exams at all, he will cram on the night before—and chances are he'll flunk. He keeps on getting into trouble but seems to learn nothing from it. He just "passes on."

An unsaved person who is simple-minded either ignores or opposes the Gospel. He lives as though there is no God, no death to die, no judgment, no eternity.

Not long ago I was driving along a major road. Suddenly another car shot out of a side street; the driver being totally oblivious to the fact that he had ignored a stop sign. I stood on my head to avoid a wreck, slamming on my brakes, turning the wheels of my car, and going into a skid. When the man driving the other car saw me he too slammed on his brakes and also went into a skid. We left rubber all over the road and ended up with our cars about a foot apart—my face looking right at his face.

When he saw me, he yelled, "Where in the blanket blankety-blank did you come from?" I started to answer, "I was born in West Palm Beach, Florida." Instead, I said, "Sir, we almost had a tragic accident. You and I could have been killed. It would have been terrible for you to go out into eternity with that kind of profanity in your heart." He snapped back, "I'll face that when I get there."

No he won't. He'll face it now, or he'll face the judgment when he gets there. The Bible makes it plain: "A prudent man foresees evil and hides himself; but the simple pass on and are punished." The simple person seems to have no comprehension of sin and of righteousness and of judgment (see John 16:8-9). The Holy Spirit came to convict of those three, but the simple person ignores the efforts of the Spirit.

Perhaps you are reading this now and answering, "I don't want to think about all that. I want to party. I don't want to talk about heaven and hell, God and judgment." "Amuse" means literally "not to think." We have a generation that is amusing itself into hell.

The simple man lives for the now. He wants to "live it up." As one song put it "I want to live fast, love hard, die young, and leave a beautiful memory." That is the anthem of the fun-loving, simpleminded person.

Many people have children and other loved ones who subscribe to that hell-hatched philosophy.

THE INSOLENCE OF THE SCORNFUL

We have considered the *ignorance of the simple*. The second step is the *insolence of the scornful*. Proverbs 1:22 asks, "How long , you simple ones, will ye love simplicity? For scorners delight in their scorning, and fools hate knowledge."

What is a scorner? If he is in junior high or high school we would call him a "smart aleck." If he is in business we would call him a cynic. If he is in art or at the university we would call him a mocker.

All of these are sidetracks for feeding his unregenerate ego. He wants to feel important, and because he lacks understanding, he must create a false air of importance. He gives off an air of "I know it all."

Notice his characteristics...

He Delights In His Scorning

Have a clean singing group show up at a coliseum, and the promoters are fortunate to break even. Have a devil-worshiping, heavy-metal band, and the simple-minded and scorners will fill up and overflow a massive amphitheater.

The scorner gets his jollies from sneering, from making fun of all that is holy, righteous, and godly. This is his gross self-fulfillment.

He Defies Instruction

Many parents have kids who have become scorners. Proverbs 13:1 teaches, "A wise son heeds his father's instruction, but a scoffer does not listen to rebuke." A favorite rejoinder is: "Get off my back. Don't preach to me," sometimes accompanied by profanity.

When you try to talk with a scorner, it is as though he is in another world. He tunes you out like switching channels on TV. You might as well carry on a conversation with a solid brick wall. He is like those Jesus spoke about who had ears to hear but heard not.

You can always tell a scorner, but you can't tell him much! Why? Because he already claims to know it all. He knows more than all the teachers in college and high school, more than his mother, his father, and more than his pastor, but in actuality he knows very little of anything but foolishness. He is just going to turn you off.

He Despises The Godly

Proverbs 15:12 explains it well: "A scoffer does not love who corrects him, nor will he go to the wise." Are you doing him a favor when you rebuke and reprove him? Hardly. The Bible indicates it is a waste of time. Never argue with a scoffer; you will not even reach first base. He will only despise you for trying to correct and reprove him.

Examine Proverbs 9:7-8: "He that corrects a scoffer a scorner gets shame for himself, and he that rebukes a wicked man only harms himself. Do not correct a scoffer, lest he hate You; rebuke a wise man, and he will love you."

It will do no good to argue with a scorner. You will merely bring humiliation upon yourself. You will have cast your pearls before swine. He will curse you; he will call you names; he will despise you.

If you are a schoolteacher or a principal, and you call such a scorner in, trying to straighten him out, he may sit there without speaking a word. But if you look into his eyes, you can read these unspoken words, "I hate your guts". The scorner hates those who try to give him instruction and wise counsel.

He delights in his scorning. He defies instruction. He will not receive it. Furthermore, *he despises the one who gave it.*

He Is Destined For Destruction

I repeat Proverbs 13:1: "A wise son heeds his father's instruction, but a scoffer does not listen to rebuke." What happens when a person will not listen to instruction? Go to verse 13a of this same chapter: "He who despises the word will be destroyed."

The scorner is going to die and go to hell. He can laugh his way en route to hell, but he cannot laugh his way out once he is there. It is tragic for a person to become a scorner.

But wait. There is help for the simple. And there may even be rescue for the scorner. While you cannot argue with the scorner, you can back off and pray for him. God may open his closed heart so you can come to him later with a "word fitly spoken," and then he may listen to you. There is a time to speak, as well as a time to be silent.

Oh, if you are the parent of a scorner, I pray that God will give you grace, patience, and wisdom. If you are a "smart-aleck" scorner (and you know if you are), I pray that God will have mercy on you, and perhaps a shaft of Gospel sunlight will come into your sin-darkened heart—and maybe you will see how dangerously you are living.

THE INTRANSIGENCE OF THE FOOL

There is hope for the simple. There is even slight hope for the scorner, but I can find little for the fool. The fool has passed the deadline. I have searched the Scriptures trying to locate the slightest scintilla of hope for the fool, but quite frankly I have found almost none. If there is hope for the outright fool, it is scant and sparse.

What are the distinguishing marks of a fool? Remember, he was simple. Then he became a scorner. Now he is a full-blown fool. He has moved from ignorance to insolence to intransigence. He has become set into a locked-in, fixed position.

He Rejects Wisdom

Let's notice the difference in the three stages. Return to Proverbs 1:22: "How long, you simple ones, will you love simplicity?" Underscore the word "love." "For scorners delight in their scorning." Underline the word "delight." They merely love and delight in their benighted situation. But notice the abrupt change. "And fools hate knowledge." The character has changed to hate. He has now become the enemy of the good and the godly.

God is the embodiment of knowledge and wisdom. The fool has become the enemy of God Himself. And what does the fool do? Number one, *he rejects wisdom.* "The fear of the LORD is the beginning of knowledge, but fools despise wisdom and instruction" (Proverbs 1:7). Worse even than a scorner, he hates the truth of God's Word. He has a perverse antipathy toward anything to do with God.

He Ridicules Righteousness

Not only does he hate wisdom, *he ridicules righteousness.* Proverbs 14:9a amazingly says, "Fools mock at sin." They laugh about sin. They ridicule it. They poke fun at preachers and teachers of righteousness.

We have raised a generation of moral miscreants who do precisely that. This nation is constantly entertained by programs laughing at sin. Pornography, homosexuality, abortion, drunkenness, divorce, infidelity, child abuse, premarital sex, and even more are the backdrop for the situation comedies people watch. Americans mock at sin.

The devil is crafty. The prince of darkness recognizes that if he can get people laughing at sin, it will then become difficult for them to ever take it seriously. Some even laugh about the devil and hell. You are certainly not going to oppose and resist a being that is the object of your mirth. So people laugh at every manner of sin—homosexuality, pornography, adultery, abortion. The devil must laugh along when people laugh about him and sin.

"Fools mock at sin." They mock at being good, being righteous, being pure. Read the entertainment pages. The producers, most of them, play on people's prurient interest. The ads depict how shocking, how sinful, how sexy, how sleazy, how sorry, how sordid the movies and TV specials have become.

He Rejoices In Sin

I am describing a fool. He rejects wisdom. He ridicules righteousness. And, three, *he rejoices in sin.* "A wise son makes a father glad, but a foolish man despises his mother. Folly is joy to him who is destitute of discernment" (Proverbs 15:20-21a). He literally enjoys his folly, his foolishness.

A simple-minded person may fall into sin. But he may have twinges of conscience over it and think, *Oh, I shouldn't have done that, and I'll try to do better.* Not so with the fool. He absolutely revels in his sin.

Why? Because his moral sense has been perverted. A poignant verse goes, "Woe to those that call evil good, and good evil; who put darkness for light, and light for darkness; who put bitter for sweet, and sweet for bitter!" (Isaiah 5:20).

What does it mean? God plainly declares that a person can reach a low point where he can no longer distinguish the difference between good and evil, right and wrong. His values become all twisted. What the Bible calls sin, he calls good.

The fool gets a kick out of sin. He glories in it. He does not know the difference between right and wrong and couldn't care less. To him there is no distinction between sweet and bitter, good and bad, and light and dark. He couldn't do good even if he wanted to, and he wouldn't know good if it wore a sign.

Woe unto the fool. He rejects wisdom. He ridicules righteousness. He rejoices in sin. Sin is his joy. He loves it. The Bible tells it like it is. Proverbs 26:11 paints a sickening picture: "As a dog returns to his own vomit, so a fool repeats his folly." What an analogy!

When a dog eats nauseous food, he has certain reflex actions, and he regurgitates that which has choked or soured within him. He vomits and walks away. But the Scripture says that the dog often returns to that mess and laps it up. Have you ever seen a dog do that? Disgusting, isn't it?

That is how sin leeches onto a foolish person. He keeps on going back to that which is destroying him and making him sick. The foolish person will lap up his sin, even though the wages of sin are putrefying. Every kick has a kickback. The fool will delve into drugs, and they will destroy him.

The history of drug-oriented rock music is filled with the horrid and early demise of many heroes and heroines—Janis Joplin, Jimmi Hendrix, Sid Vicious, ad nauseum. They kept going back until it killed them.

He Is Headed For Destruction

A simple-minded person is ignorant; a mocker is insolent; but a fool is intransigent, fixed, immovable. There seems to be no hope for him because *he is headed for destruction.* Proverbs 17:10 observes, "Rebuke is more effective for a wise man than a hundred blows to a fool."

It appears you can rebuke and punish a fool again and again, but you are probably not going to change him. Punishment probably will not transform him. Prison will not alter him. That is why so many people like this keep going back to jail and prison. He will still be a fool, even when he is released.

Many parents have come to the conclusion, *Good grief, I have raised a fool, but I'm going to change him now. I'm going to straighten him out.* And they have tried to beat that fool, physically and/or verbally, but it still does not change his heart. A hundred stripes on his back will not do it. You can beat him to his knees, but you'll never change him. He'll die in his foolishness. He has become an ingrained fool, hating righteousness, not knowing the difference between right and wrong, and loving his foolishness—wallowing in it.

Pharaoh was a fool. God sent one judgment after another. Do you think ten plagues changed him? The Bible states that he hardened his heart more and more. Pharaoh is in hell today because he was a fool.

A child starts out simple. Then he becomes scornful. And finally he becomes foolish. *So how do you as a parent intervene in this process before it becomes too late?* You've probably been asking that question since the beginning of this chapter—right? What hope is there?

Now that we have delineated "the anatomy of a fool," let's look at the Scriptures from another viewpoint. *Let me share with you how not to raise a fool.*

HOW NOT TO RAISE A FOOL

Teach Him God's Word

Number one, *remember that the simple can be taught.* Proverbs 1:1-4 (KJV) declares, "The proverbs of Solomon the son of David, king of Israel; to know wisdom and instruction, to perceive the words of understanding, to receive the instruction of wisdom, justice, judgment, and equity; to give subtlety to the simple...."

"Subtlety" here means wisdom, understanding, and discernment; if you please, "savvy." And God has given us a book. It is the book of Proverbs—to help simple children become wise ones. Remember parents, that a child can be taught if you start early enough to give him the Word of God.

The Bible teaches that we should give subtlety to the simple and to the "young man," the young person. Many of you started about two hundred pounds and sixteen years too late. From the time they are children you had better begin to put the Word of God into them.

Every parent ought to master the book of Proverbs and be mastered by that book, so they can learn how to teach their children. That is one of the major reasons God presented us this book. It is His manual on child rearing. This is God's book to tell us how not to raise a fool. The wisdom of God is in its pages.

Do you know God's Word? Are you actually qualified to instill these truths into your children? Remember the word simple. It means open, and the child is open to God's Word as well as he is open to anything else. God gave him to you with a plastic, pliable mentality. He can be taught when he is "simple." But he must be taught early.

Show Him By Example

Second, remember *that he learns by example.* Proverbs 19:25a says: "Smite a scoffer, and the simple will become wary." Isn't that perceptive? The simple learns from seeing the scoffer punished.

A mother reported to a little boy's schoolteacher: "Now, Johnny is nervous. If he misbehaves, you slap the boy next to him, and Johnny will straighten up." There's a smidgen of truth in that. "Smite the scoffer, and the simple will become wary." Again, let me show you. "When the scoffer is punished, the simple is made wise" (Proverbs 21:11a).

If you have a child who is simple, and who does not have serious thoughts, you need to show him every time when sin is punished. When a teenager is killed by drunk driving, you might consider taking the simple to the funeral, even though you may not know the deceased. You ought to read the news to him. You must show him what the Bible teaches about the wages of sin.

Without your help, your child is probably going to think very little about these matters. "A prudent man foresees evil and hides himself, but the simple pass on and are punished" (Proverbs 22:3). They will not understand unless you teach them.

What is dangerous for the simple-minded child? To be raised in a permissive society—and your children are being brought up in such a place. "Anything Goes" might just as well have been written today as in 1934. Sin is not punished fairly and swiftly in this kind of environment.

Ecclesiastes 8:11 notes: "Because the sentence against an evil work is not executed speedily, therefore the heart of the sons of men is fully set in them to do evil." If people were arrested, brought to trial, quickly judged, sentenced, and punished with dispatch, the crime rate would nosedive. By your example and your teaching, you will have to offset the permissiveness of our society.

We have heard most of the axioms about big oaks growing from the little acorns. It is true. King Solomon laid it down: "Train up a child in the way he should go, and when he is old he will not depart from it" (Proverbs 22:6).

As unappetizing as it may seem, you are to point out the bad aspects in our society in addition to the good. Show him what happens to the alcoholic. Do not let him be brainwashed by the beer and wine advertisements on TV. Drive or walk him through skid row. Show him the drunk lying in his excrement and vomit and covered with flies. Carry him to the drug rehabilitation center, and let him have a look at those hollow-cheeked and pale-faced kids on dope.

When the scorner is smitten, the simple will learn. The child, the simple one, learns by example.

Awhile back, the *CBS Evening News* featured an illuminating report concerning an approach by Judge Jeffrey L. Gunther, Judge of the Municipal Court of Sacramento, California. Judge Gunther received an avalanche of phone calls and mail from across the nation commending him for his unusual method of dealing with youthful DUI offenders. I was one of those who wrote him. He graciously sent me a personal letter and a stack of correspondence from counselors and law enforcement officers from every section of the country.

He wrote: "I have enclosed a recent article from our local newspaper which describes the operation of the program. Essentially those convicted or who plead guilty to a first time DUI receive a standard DUI sentence which at a minimum is 60 days in jail suspended for a term of 3 years summary probation under the following terms and conditions of probation:

1. Not drink alcoholic beverages at all until reaching the age of 21.

2. After age 21, not drive a motor vehicle with any measurable amount of alcohol in their system.

3. Not refuse to take a blood alcohol chemical test when offered by any peace officer.
4. Obey all laws.
5. Not drive a motor vehicle without a valid California Driver License in their possession at all times.
6. Serve 2 days in the County Jail (on occasion in lieu I will approve two 8-hour workdays on the Sheriff's Work Program painting schools or picking up litter on roads and parks).
7. Pay restitution if involved in an accident.
8. Pay fine of $827.00 or serve an additional 16 days of jail time or work project in lieu.
9. Visit the emergency room at our County Medical Center between the hours of 10 PM and 2 AM on a Friday or Saturday night to observe the victims of auto accidents involving the drinking driver. In addition, a tour of the hospital's Acute Care Clinic for alcoholics in the terminal stages of their disease is provided.
10. Visit the County Coroner's office to observe appropriate victims of auto accidents involving the drinking driver.
11. At the conclusion of these visits a personal visit with the young persons and their attorney and/or parents in my chambers to discuss the young persons' experiences and how they will impact on future conduct. As an alternative for those who are away from Sacramento at school or work, a 1,000-word essay on this topic may be substituted. These essays describe the program from the view of the defendant. I have enclosed a few for your perusal that I believe are representative.

"At this point in time over 150 young people have received this sentence. The results have been very encouraging. At this time I am not aware of any repeat offenders... I still consider the program to be experimental. I personally attribute the success of the program to Nurse Barbara Leary and Chief Deputy Coroner Robert Bowers..."

A business executive wrote Judge Gunther: "I thought you might be interested in knowing that twenty years ago, when I was eighteen, I worked in an emergency room of a large municipal hospital. I would recommend the experience to anyone who is inclined to ride a motorcycle or to drink and drive."

One woman from North Carolina wrote: "Your sentence to young offenders of the drinking and driving laws is outstanding. It is the most sensitive, caring, rational and creative approach to any offense, of which I have ever heard. May God bless your approach."

Several states and municipalities have written asking for additional information, statistics, and how to implement Judge Gunther's approach.

Judge Gunther sent me sixteen of the essays. The kids were horrified and shocked after visiting the emergency room, the County Coroner's morgue, and the Acute Care Clinic for alcoholics, not to mention being arrested, handcuffed, and placed in a cell with other DUI offenders.

One wrote: "I was soon placed in a large cell with everybody else who had committed an alcohol-related crime that evening... All the other men in the cell were larger than me, and most could have easily crushed me if that was what they desired. Although I was tired there was no way I would fall asleep like so many other people were doing. I sat in fear for six hours before finally being released.

"While visiting the county medical center emergency room, I watched an unsuccessful attempt to revive a car accident victim, indeed, this person could easily have been me, or worse yet the person I crashed into. After this person was wheeled into one of the emergency rooms, his bloody clothes were removed and discarded onto the floor. The huge hole in his chest was now fully exposed and in plain view of my eyesight... I had just witnessed the loss of human life for the first time."

Another said (about his visit to the morgue): "Mr. Bowers opened the door, I could see about twenty to thirty bodies covered under white linen. He then guided me to one particular body that was set in the center of the room. He uncovered the body. I saw this lifeless body that was once a living person less than twenty-four hours earlier. The face of the body was very disturbing. His eyes were blackened all the way around. His head shaven, with staples replacing stitches that closed incisions. Mr. Bowers explained that the person was killed by a drunk driver while crossing the street."

By now, perhaps you are answering me, "How crude. How coarse. How can Adrian suggest such as that?" But wouldn't you rather your child see the results of alcohol than to end up an alcoholic? Wouldn't you rather carry your kid to the rehab place for a visit than for him to end up there himself or worse?

Many men who came along in my age group were in the military. Part of their early training was a barrage of films on clean living, especially about the dangers of venereal disease. Those films were so sickening and graphic that many a man made up his mind, *I'm not going to play around. I'm going to keep myself clean in the military and later in civilian life.*

Guard His Company

Third, *guard his company.* "He who walks with wise men will be wise, but the companion of fools will be destroyed" (Proverbs 13:20). Let him get mad and protest, "Why do you want to know who I'm with? You don't like my friends, and it's not any of your business." Oh, yes it is. Don't let him keep company with fools because he is so open, so susceptible. Just plain gullible.

Proverbs 22:10 advises, "Cast out the scoffer, and contention will leave; yes, strife and reproach will cease." There is a time to expel a kid from school. Cast him out—not cast him off. You still love him, pray for him. But you cannot allow the scorner or the fool to pull down the simple. The Bible declares for us to cast him out. There is a time when people ought to be put away from society, to be expelled from school, to be "disfellowshipped" from churches because they are unrepentant troublemakers. We are to love them and pity them, but we are to disassociate from them.

Choose your children's friends and choose them carefully. Choose them when they are young, and let your children invite their friends into your home. Rather than fussing about them messing up the house, you should rejoice that they want to invite their young friends home. Make them welcome but also check them out. If one of them is a scorner, say firmly but kindly, "Son, there's the sidewalk. Get on it. I'm afraid you're not welcome here."

You reply, "That's hard." Listen, God gave you those children, and you had better protect them. You had better care for them. "The companion of fools shall be destroyed."

What seems to mean more to a teenager than all else? And I almost hate to hear the term—it is bandied about all the time—peer pressure. Their religion is the code of conformity, and their chief hymn is, "Everybody's doing it, doing it, doing it." If you dare to be different, that is considered a "sin" among many teenagers.

The Bible still warns us about bad companions. There is hardly a kid who picked up bad habits in a vacuum by himself. He heard, "Hey, try this. Take a puff. It's cool." Or, "Man, you're not 'in' if you don't drink." Or, "You're a nerd if you're a virgin." Etc. Etc. Etc. Yet, on the other hand God says, "He that walketh with wise men shall be wise."

Peer pressure, "the herd instinct," can be fantastic if you help surround your kids with good, solid, Christian peers. Even then, make sure they have the right influence. You can work with your kids on this situation of peer pressure. A wise parent uses the leverage of peer pressure.

One unnamed sage observed that there are four categories of people. There is the man who knows not, and cares not that he knows not. He is a fool. Avoid him. There is the man who knows not, but knows not that he knows not. He is simple. Teach him. There is the man who knows, but has forgotten that he knows. He is asleep. Awake him. And there is the man who knows and knows that he knows. He is a wise man. Follow him.

In *One Home Under God,* Jack R. Taylor has written:

> Parents, yours is a serious vocation. If you shirk it, the expense will be high and will continue for generations. To do the job as it should be done will take more than your money, your time, and your planning. It will take *you*! It will take you... totally involved and totally available... not only to your family, but to God. It is not a job you can do by yourself. You cannot love without God in the manner which the task requires. In proper patterns within the home, the child will be the benefactor of the flow of divine life according to God's order. When authority is as it should be, God is pleased to move, bless and dwell where it is happening. As this happens, all will become aware of God's love and abundant life. Every promise in the Word of God is not only a personal promise, but a promise for the family. Jesus said, "I come that they might have life, and that they might have it more abundantly" (John 10:10). This is for your family and mine.[1]

---

1. Jack R. Taylor, *One Home Under God* (Nashville, TN: Broadman & Holman Publishers, 1974), p. 70.

Parent, with the young ones it is still not too late. With the scorning ones there is a scant chance. With the foolish ones there is practically no hope.

Why not vow before God, if it is not too late, "Lord, by Your grace and the power of the Holy Spirit, use me that my children may be wise according to Your Word." "For what shall it profit a man if he gain the whole world, but lose his own son?"

CHAPTER FOUR

FINDING GOD'S WAY IN A DARK DAY

Trust in the LORD with all your heart, and lean not on your own understanding; in all your ways acknowledge Him, and He shall direct your paths. (Proverbs 3:5-6)

M an is a clever creature, but he has lost his way in the darkness. If you are fifty years or younger you have experienced countless amazing breakthroughs and a breathtaking unlocking of knowledge in your lifetime.

In your day scientists have split the atom and created nuclear devices that are capable of destroying life as we know it on planet Earth. In your lifetime space travel has become a reality, not merely a "pipedream" of Buck Rogers and Flash Gordon comic strips of the 1930s and later. United States astronauts have left their spaceboot tracks on the moon.

Your great-grandfather would have argued that such was not only improbable but also impossible. We have made the trip to the moon, not on the songwriter's "gossamer wings" but in a spacecraft— and our ships have made probes to Venus, Mars, and the regions beyond.

As always Bible prophecy is coming true. The Word predicted that in the last days men would rush "to and fro" in accelerated activity and discovery. We have automobiles that can travel 600 MPH (and some kids try to do that on the roads and highways!), airplanes that travel 2,000 MPH, and spacecraft that reach 24,000 MPH or more.

A man asked a clerk (I am told) at the Memphis International Airport, "How long does it take to fly from Memphis to Dallas?" The busy clerk replied, "Just a minute." The man said, "Thank you," and walked away.

We may arrive there faster, but we still have no idea where we are going. About all we have added is speed and noise. And all this has happened within the last fifty years!

Yet in those same years, divorce has increased from one in twenty marriages to one in two marriages! Crime has skyrocketed 700 percent. Yes, man is truly a clever, inventive creature... but he has lost his bearings in a chaotic world.

Forty years ago, at the close of World War II, General Douglas MacArthur predicted: "We have had our last chance. If we do not now devise some greater and more equitable system, Armageddon will be at our door. The problem basically is theological and involves a spiritual recrudescence and improvement of human character... It must be of the spirit if we are to save the flesh."

But in the middle of this midnight of despair shines God's promise, "The LORD will guide you continually" (Isaiah 58:11a). Psalm 32:8 assures us, "I will instruct you and teach you in the way you should go; I will guide you with My eye."

We do not have to be misguided in an age of guided missiles. "For we are His workmanship, created in Christ Jesus for good works, which God prepared beforehand that we should walk in them" (Ephesians 2:10).

Is it hard for you to believe? God has a master plan for your life that He laid before the foundation of the world. He not only has a plan for nations and churches—but He has a definite plan for individuals. You and me.

One old song went, "Since before time began, you were part of His plan." God is so intimately concerned with you that "the very hairs of your head are all numbered" (Matthew 10:30). And if you are bald, He numbers the hair follicles and the pores of your skin!

"The steps of a good man are ordered by the LORD, and He delights in his way" (Psalm 37:23). If you have Christ as your Lord and Savior, not only is your entire life ordered, but every single step within that life. God has a plan for the plumber as well as the preacher, for the electrician as well as the evangelist, for the mechanic as well as the missionary. And if God calls you to be a plumber, for instance, and you end up being a preacher, you are accepting second best!

To do God's will is the highest achievement of any person. Success is not spelled m-o-n-e-y. Neither is it spelled *f-a-m-e* (even though there was a musical and a movie by that name).

Success rather is the continuous realization of the will of God— what God desires, what God wants—for your life. And because God does have a plan for you, you would certainly expect Him to reveal that plan to you.

Our duty, our privilege, and our exciting thrill is to find the will of God, follow that will, and finish it—so that when we come to the last period upon the last page of our lives, we can testify, "I have finished the work You gave me to do, O Lord." And God can commend you, "Well done, good and faithful servant... enter into the joy of your Lord" (see Matthew 25:23). That is success! Having the approval and commendation of our Lord is the greatest!!!

Remember that God has a will for your individual life. God does not make copies or clones—only originals. There is a will for me and a will for you. And the ultimate purpose of our lives is mainly one, and that is to be like Jesus.

> Beloved, now are we children of God; and it has not yet been revealed what we shall be, but we know that when He is revealed, we shall be like Him, for we shall see Him as He is. (1 John 3:2)

We used to sing in college days, "To Be Like Jesus." There it is. God's overriding purpose for us is that we are "being conformed to His death" (Philippians 3:10c). Ah, but God has as many methods as He has men. Those methods are individual—and amazing.

How do you let God direct your life, leading you to find and follow and finish His "good and acceptable and perfect will of God" (Romans 12:2c)?

THERE SHOULD BE A TRUSTING CONFIDENCE

Trust in the LORD with all your heart, and lean not on your own understanding. (Proverbs 3:5)

There it is. "Trust in the LORD." I have no other scheme to which you are to subscribe no other plan, philosophy, or program. Have you noticed the number of "isms" and "schisms" these esoteric systems have? Or how many of these cults make weird, complicated demands on their followers? And people, like lemmings, running for the cliff, follow some twisted guru.

I am asking you to trust a Person, the Lord Jesus Christ, the One altogether lovely. To discern His will, you do not have to put your body into all kinds of contortions or sell flowers on the street corners or make strange sounds or chants. Simply "trust in the LORD with all thine heart." He is the King of kings and the Lord of lords.

Many find it difficult just to trust the Lord and lean on Him. Why? If they are having difficulty trusting in Him, it is because they do not love Him. You see, you cannot trust a person you do not love.

Has a stranger ever asked you, "Hey, will you do something for me?" The first question out of your mouth probably was: "Well what is it?" And if that stranger answered, "Never mind what it is—just trust me." I am sure you explained, "Look, I really need to know you better in order to trust you."

But suppose my darling wife, Joyce, comes to me and inquires, "Adrian, will you do something for me?" Knowing me, my first question will still probably be, "What is it, Honey?" But if she were to say, "Never mind—just trust me," I would. I love her enough and know her enough to realize she loves me enough never to ask anything that would harm or embarrass me or put me in a position that would not be in my best interests.

I could agree, "Yes, Joyce, I will do it," because I love her. If I did not love her, it would be hard for me to trust her.

But wait. We are not ready to move on. You do not know the Lord if you do not love Him. If you did know Him you would love Him because He is altogether lovely. You could not possibly know Him without loving Him.

And you do not know Him because you are not spending time with Him. There is no real love at first sight. There may be infatuation, but it is only through love that trust develops. And as that trust develops, then obedience is nurtured. And when obedience is nurtured, blessing always ensues.

- To know Him is to love Him.
- To love Him is to trust Him.
- To trust Him is to obey Him.
- To obey Him is to be blessed!

Notice again the phrase in Proverbs 3:5: "And lean not on your own understanding." I want to make it crystal-clear: the Bible does not lead us to believe we are to be without understanding. God wants us to understand, but He does not want us to lean on our own understanding. Proverbs 3:7 advises, "Be not wise in thine own eyes." The reason is: "There is a way that sees right to a man, but its end is the ways of death" (Proverbs 14:12).

One may have consulted his doctor and his banker and his own intellect. He may have looked at all the factors and thought he had it all figured out. But the Bible still says that the end is the way of death. Jeremiah 10:23b says, "It is not in man who walks to direct his own steps." Yet we are to have understanding:

> So that you incline your ear to wisdom, and apply your heart to understanding; Yes, if you cry out for discernment, and lift up your voice for understanding, if you seek her as silver, and search for her as for hidden treasures; Then you will understand the fear of the LORD, and find the knowledge of God. For the LORD gives wisdom; from His mouth come knowledge and understanding. (Proverbs 2:2-6)

God is not saying we are not to use the sanctified wisdom He gives. He is teaching us, though, that we are not to trust our own understanding without leaning on Him. We are not to be wise in our own sight. He wants us to operate with His wisdom and His understanding. And that is remarkably wonderful.

THERE MUST BE A TOTAL COMMITMENT

> In all your ways acknowledge Him, and He shall direct your paths. (Proverbs 3:6)

God asks for a complete commitment to Him which acknowledges Him as Lord over every area of your life. You are to acknowledge Him as the One whose right it is to rule over your life. Acknowledge Him in your business, in your recreation, in your home, in your worship, in everything. In all—not merely some—of your ways, you are to acknowledge Him.

You need to sign a blank check and give it to God. You need to sign a contract at the bottom and commit yourself, "Here it is God. You fill in the details."

One of my favorite preachers is Dr. Stephen Olford, a man mighty in the Scriptures. Dr. Olford was raised in Africa, the son of missionary parents. He was a brilliant boy, and he decided he wanted to pursue a course in engineering. He went away to one of the finest schools in all of the world where he received the equivalent of straight As. His plan was to become successful, to have leisure, to accumulate the "nice things" money could buy, and with his wealth he could help the missionaries and the Word of God on the side. It seemed like a splendid plan to him, but unfortunately it was one he worked out in his own mind.

It was all set, but then he became deathly sick. He went to the doctor and was put to bed. The doctor gravely intoned, "Young man, in two weeks you will be dead."

Stephen's life caved in around him. But a letter came from his missionary father who had no way of knowing his son's condition because of the time lag in the mail delivery from overseas. In that letter his dad wrote those touching words you and I have heard so many times:

'Tis one life, 'Twill soon be past.
Only what's done for Christ will last.

In the stillness of that room God broke through. Stephen bowed his head and prayed a brief prayer, "Anywhere, anytime, any cost. Amen."

Would you be willing to pray that prayer? Or would you be afraid? If you are afraid of Him, it is because you don't love Him. And if you don't love Him, it is because you don't know Him, and if you don't know Him, it is because you have not been spending time getting acquainted with Him.

Do not be afraid of His will. The will of God is not something you have to do—it is something you get to do as a privilege. God will choose for you something that you would choose for yourself if you had enough sense to choose it.

I realize you are thinking, But I may end up in Africa as a missionary. Ah, but if that is God's will for you, you should be unhappy being anywhere else. Like the poet, you ought to say, "Like a bird that found his nest, So my soul has found its rest, In the center of the will of God."

Never slander the character of God by making it seem like the only choice you have is between doing the will of God on one hand or "fulfillment" on the other. If you delight yourself in the Lord, He will give you the desires of your heart (see Psalm 37:4). Our own Lord said, "My food is to do the will of Him who sent Me" (John 4:34a). This is the only real source of real satisfaction and real fulfillment.

THERE WILL BE A THRILLING CONSEQUENCE

And He shall direct your paths. (Proverbs 3:6b)

No ifs, ands, or buts about it. He will do it. There will be a divine direction, and that is sublime, but coupled with it will be a divine dynamic, and that is fabulous.

When you realize this, and if it doesn't excite you, then you have bunions on your soul. Pay attention. There is going to be a divine direction. God is going to point, "This is the way, walk in it" (Isaiah 30:21b). How will He direct you and speak to you?

Through His Word

"Your word is a lamp to my feet and a light to my path" (Psalm 119:105). A considerable amount of God's will has already been revealed. This includes the moral choices you have to make.

Sometimes a man will come to me for counseling and confide, "Pastor, you know I am married to so and so. But I really feel that it is God's will for me to divorce her and marry this other woman. Would you pray with me about it?"

Of course, I won't pray with him about it. There is no need to pray about it. God is not going to change His Holy Word for that man or anyone else who is looking for an "out." The Bible makes it plain, "You shall not commit adultery" (Exodus 20:14).

Some people identify with the man who stood up in the church business meeting, read the Scriptures, and absentmindedly blurted out, "If there are no additions or corrections to the Scripture reading, it will stand approved as read." Friend, they stand—period. And if you would follow God's will, you must know its clear teachings.

Through Revelation To Our Heart

There are some who do not believe God speaks supernaturally to the inner man. With all my heart I believe He does. God will speak by communicating to our spirits.

For example, after Judas fell by transgression, the apostles wanted to learn who should take Judas' place. "And they prayed and said, 'You, O Lord, who knows the hearts of all, show which of these two You have chosen'" (Acts 1:24). God speaks to hearts and gives direction when we pray. Of course He will never reveal anything not in keeping with His Word.

Many times He speaks in the quietness of the heart. That is why we must understand that prayer is a two-way street. You do not pray at God—you talk *with* God.

Have you ever been in a conversation when one person does all the talking? It really isn't a conversation, is it? It's only a monologue. Someone has quipped, "An egotist is somebody who talks about himself so much you don't have time to talk about yourself."

Too many times we come to God almost commanding, "Listen, Lord, your servant speaks," rather than, "Speak, Lord, for your servant hears." Many times we do not become quiet and let the still small voice of God's Holy Spirit speak to our spirit.

Another example of God speaking to our hearts is found in Acts 8:29, "Then the Spirit said unto Philip, 'Go near, and join thyself to this chariot'". How do you think the Spirit said that? Do you think He yelled, "Hey, Philip, this is the Lord. Go over there."? No. Philip was in tune, he was in the stream of the Spirit, and he was impressed in his heart to go.

Again in Acts 13:2, the church was praying, seeking God's will about spreading the Word, and, "As they ministered to the Lord and fasted, the Holy Spirit said, 'Now separate Me Barnabas and Saul for the work to which I have called them'". The great missionary enterprise of Paul and Barnabas was begun when the Spirit of God gave a corporate consensus as He moved upon the hearts of the church members.

Nehemiah wanted to ascertain God's will about the vast building program God had set before the people. He pointed out, "Then my God put into my heart to gather together the nobles, the rulers, and the people" (Nehemiah 7:5a). God has a plan, and He planted that plan in the heart of Nehemiah.

Through Wisdom

"If any of you lack wisdom, let him ask of God, who gives to all men liberally and without reproach, and it will be given to him. But let him ask in faith, with no doubting" (James 1:5-6a).

This is a major premise of this book—*God's Wisdom Is Better Than Gold.* "Let him ask of God... and it will be given him." Wisdom is yours for the asking. What is this wisdom God gives? It is not simply feeling warm around the heart and wet around the lashes. It is not merely goose-bumps and shivers of the liver. Wisdom is sanctified common sense. Wisdom is having the mind of Christ—looking at life from Jesus' perspective. It is knowing and applying the principles of God's Word.

Dr. Donald Gray Barnhouse said, "I'm convinced that 90 percent of the will of God is found above the neck." According to the Bible, we are to appeal to God for this kind of wisdom.

We can understand the will of God for our lives. "Therefore do not be unwise, but understand what the will of the Lord is" (Ephesians 5:17). First Corinthians 10:15 says, "I speak as to wise men; judge for yourselves what I say."

That is, use your intellect on fire with the Holy Spirit. Develop the mind of Christ, and you will think the thoughts of Christ after Him.

> Among the things that this day brings
> Will come to you a call,
> The which, unless you're listening,
> You may not hear at all;
> Lest it be very soft and low,
> Whate'er you do, where'er you go,
> Be listening.
> When God shall come and say to you,

"Here is the thing that you must do,"
　　Be listening.

Through Providence

"These things says He who is holy, He who is true, He who has the key of David, He who opens and no one shuts, and shuts and no one opens" (Revelation 3:7). God will make certain things possible and others, impossible. But that does not mean the possible things are going to be easy. It has been aptly expressed, "The door to the room of opportunity swings on the hinges of opposition."

Paul himself wrote, "There is an open, and there are many adversaries" (see 1 Corinthians 16:9). Even when the door is open, the devil and his cohorts will heatedly oppose you. There may be blood, sweat, and tears. But, praise God, when He does open a door, there is not a demon in hell or out that can shut that door!

God does "lead His dear children along" and He does the leading in different ways—but here is the hallelujah part. That word "direct," the Hebrew word *yashur*, literally means to cut a path or to clear the way. Some translations read, "He shall make thy paths straight." Or "He shall make your paths smooth." That is the literal rendering of *yashur*.

The idea is not only of leading, but of leading by "clearing the way" as a trailblazer or a pathfinder. It is the same phrase used in Isaiah 40:3-4 where, speaking of John the Baptist, it prophesies, "The voice of one crying in the wilderness, Prepare the way of the LORD; make straight in the desert a highway for our God. Every valley shall be exalted, and every mountain and hill brought low; the crooked places shall be made straight, and the rough places smooth."

For the person who faithfully trusts God and acknowledges Him in all of his ways, God will bulldoze a path through the wilderness! That is exactly the meaning of "He shall direct thy paths." "Cut a path." Mountains will melt and valleys will be filled. Crooked places will be straightened out and rough places will be smoothed out by the power of God.

We sing, "My Lord knows the way through the wilderness, all you have to do is follow." The Lord clears the way through the wilderness. No man, no demon, no force, no power can withstand the people of God when they are walking in the Holy Spirit. If you do not believe that, close your Bible and never read it again. You ought to withdraw from the whole business, because, if the devil is greater than Christ in us, then we are on the wrong team.

But no one can stand against the Holy Spirit as He energizes the people of God. The power of Christ in us is exciting beyond human words of expression. There is divine direction wed together with a divine dynamic. God is the Bulldozer, the Pathfinder, the Trailblazer, the Explorer, and the Guide for those who love Him.

No wonder Christians can sing, "If Jesus goes with me, I'll go anywhere!" Because He will not only go with us, He will go before us to clear the pathway. He will run the interference and do the downfield blocking.

How are you going to know and do God's will for your life?

God's will is not a road map—it is a relationship. Let that seize you. "In all thy ways acknowledge Him." "Trust in the Lord." I am happy it is not a road map. I am grateful to God He does not specify to me, "Now, Adrian five years from now you are going to be doing thus and so. Then ten years from now you are going to be doing this or that. And fifteen years..."

That might be boring. It would leave no room for God's serendipities. It could also lead to considerable grief if we knew far ahead the suffering which was waiting down the pike. There is romance in serving Christ. All I have to do is to know Him and follow Him as He impresses my heart today.

I'm not worried about tomorrow. I follow Him today, and today then turns into tomorrow. The way to find God's will for the rest of your life is to do God's will for the next fifteen minutes!

A man confided, "I have been called to be a missionary."

His friend asked, "Well, what are you doing for the Lord now?"

The man answered, "Not much."

His friend ended the interchange: "Then please don't go overseas and do it."

"He who is faithful in what is least is faithful also in much" (Luke 16:10a). If you are not doing His will in the small and everyday things, why should God reveal to you the big things?

"Trust in the Lord with all your heart; and lean not on your own understanding. In all your ways acknowledge Him, and He shall direct your paths."

An unknown poet wrote:

I may not always know the way
Wherein God leads my feet;
But this I know, that 'round my path
His love and wisdom meet,
And so I rest content to know
He guides my feet where'er they go.

May you find God's way in a dark day.

CHAPTER FIVE

A CHECKUP FROM THE NECK UP

Keep your heart with all diligence, for out of it spring the issues of life. Put away from you a deceitful mouth, and put perverse lips far from you. Let your eyes look straight ahead, and let your eyelids look right before you. Ponder the path of your feet, and let all your ways be established.
(Proverbs 4:23-26)

W arning! Your thought life may be hazardous to your health. The word "heart" is used more than eight hundred times in the Old Testament. More than two hundred of those times it deals with the thought life, not merely the intelligence but the emotions, the wellsprings of life, that which motivates us and moves us.

It is roughly equivalent to what the New Testament calls the mind. So Proverbs 4:23 could just as easily read, "Keep your mind, keep your thought life with all diligence; for out of it are the issues of life."

Therefore, we need to pay attention to our hearts, to our thought lives. Solomon instructed his son to keep his heart with all diligence because of...

THE MAJESTY OF THE THOUGHT LIFE

Your thought life, according to Solomon, controls the rest of your life. "Out of it are the issues of life." What occupies your thoughts and captivates your imagination? All too many think in terms of the lust of the flesh and the lust of the eye and the pride of life (see 1 John 2:15-17). They are obsessed with carnality and banality, the trivia of the world.

Proverbs 23:7a makes it manifestly clear: "For as he thinks in his heart, so is he." It goes to the core of the life. Your thought life dominates and shapes your attitudes, whether positive or negative, good or bad. Your attitudes are merely the sum total of your thoughts.

Because your attitudes lead to your actions, watch out. The thought is the father of the deed. Before you can do this or that, somewhere it has to cross your mind, your thought processes. So the heart leads to the attitude, and the attitude leads to the action, and the action leads to the achievement.

The achievements of your life are going to be the sum total of your thoughts. An anonymous author mused:

> Sow a thought,
> Reap an act;
> Sow an act,
> Reap a habit;
> Sow a habit,
> Reap a character;
> Sow a character,
> Reap a destiny!

It all begins with the thought life.

This is so basic, so fundamental. Once God destroyed an entire civilization simply because they had "heart trouble."

> Then the LORD saw the wickedness of man was great in the earth, and that every intent of the thoughts of his heart was only evil continually. And the LORD was sorry that He had made man on the earth, and He was grieved in His heart. So the LORD said, I will destroy man whom I have created from the face of the earth; both man and beast, creeping

thing and birds of the air, for I am sorry that I have made them. (Genesis 6:5-7)

Notice—"every intent of the thoughts of his heart was only evil continually." The flood in the time of Noah was because of men's hearts.

It is still true today. The heart of the human problem is the problem of the human heart. Matthew 24:37 says, "But as the days of Noah were, so also will the coming of the Son of man be." To this day the deeply ingrained problem has not changed.

God saw that the thoughts, the evil imaginations of men's hearts, ultimately led to certain degradation. And those degradations were so vile and disgusting that God had to destroy them.

Conversely, when God prepares to mold a man and motivate a man He does it by changing how that man thinks. The initial meaning of the New Testament word translated "repentance" is *metanoia*, meaning to change one's mind. When a person repents, he changes his mind about himself and his sin, about his condition, and about God.

Romans 12:2a implores, "And do not be conformed to this world, but be transformed by the renewing of your mind..." God transforms you by changing your thought processes. When God is in the heart, then a person is enabled to think right, live right, and do right. But when God is refused, a person thinks wrong, lives wrong, and does wrong.

Therefore, a fierce battle is being waged for the control of our minds. Is your mind a sanctuary or a cesspool? What dominates your thoughts? The devil claws to influence the mind of a believer. He cannot possess the Christian, but he can make him miserable. The devil wants to bombard our minds with his distortions whether it is the thought of foolishness, concocting a falsehood, thinking evil thoughts of others, or catering to lustful scenarios.

The Lord Jesus longs for you to present your heart and mind thoroughly to Him, along with your thought patterns.

Fifteen prominent college professors took this challenge: "If all the books on the art of moving human beings into action were condensed into one brief statement, what would that statement be?" The result of their deliberations was:

What the mind attends to,
    it considers;

What the mind does not attend to,
    it dismisses.
What the mind attends to continually,
    it believes.
What the mind believes,
    it eventually does.[2]

THE MASTERY OF THE THOUGHT LIFE

In essence, Solomon was instructing his son, "Son, guard your life of thoughts. Protect your thought patterns. Be careful about what is allowed to traipse across your mind." The mind is the battleground between Christ and Satan. The Christian must be on the alert.

How are you going to do it? How are you going to be able to conquer evil thoughts, lustful thoughts, errant thoughts which rob God of His glory and praise? It is obvious. In order to think pure thoughts, you have to carefully control and select what enters your mind.

At this point, let me explain that it is impossible to keep every sinful thought from assaulting our minds. Perhaps you have accidentally seen or heard this or that and had absolutely no control over it. You tried to brush it aside as quickly as it arrived—perhaps it was a dirty joke you could not avoid hearing or it was a photo you never expected to see. Or you heard evil gossip about another person.

The context of this particular passage concerns the sexual affairs of a young man, and Solomon is warning his son not to allow impure, immoral thoughts into his heart and life. This verse pleading for the son to guard his mind is part of that whole train of thought in chapter 5 which speaks of the heartbreak of immorality. Today we call those concepts "pornography."

Pornography comes from the two Greek words *porne*, meaning whore, and *graphe*, meaning writing. It means "the writing of a whore." Pornography is a hell-originated philosophy which teaches that sex can be divorced from love, from commitment, from morality, and from responsibility. It is the hellish belief that you can take sex alone, use it, and enjoy it apart from the guidelines set down by Almighty God, and still be successful. You cannot.

---

2. Nelson L. Price, *How to Find Out Who You Are* (Nashville, TN: Broadman & Holman Publishers, 1977), p.48.

A veritable sewer pipe has broken throughout our nation. In 1996 Americans bought an estimated eight billion dollars worth of pornography—books, tapes, films, gadgets. That is more than the legitimate music and film industry combined. Can you imagine the harm being done to our nation?

It ought to break our hearts, but instead it is producing immunity and insensitivity. What was horrible yesterday seems acceptable today and is becoming a steppingstone for that which is worse tomorrow.

Certain people will tell you, "Oh, what you see doesn't affect you." If that is true, then why do companies spend over $1 million for a half-minute commercial slot during the Super Bowl? Yes, what you see will affect you and ultimately change you. What you let into your heart and mind has to come back out in some way. And you are the sum total of the thoughts that compute into your mind. That is why we have many stern warnings against sexual sin throughout the book of Proverbs.

Pornography Is A Psychological Poison

Dr. Victor Kline, professor of psychology at the University of Utah, stated that in his fifteen years of private practice, dealing with many people who had been enmeshed and entangled in pornography, he had observed basically four steps in the psychological poisoning of a person.

Step one, he said, is the addiction factor. Unless a man is careful, he cannot just look and walk away. Pornography is like a powerful drug that puts its hooks and claws into your brain.

Step two is the escalation factor. That is, what thrills him, what titillates him, what turns him on must become a little rougher, a little dirtier, a little more deviant.

Step three is the desensitization factor. No longer does the porn addict see baseness and grossness as shocking. No longer does he see them as brutal, as evil. He begins to think of perversity as normal and right. Rather than being repulsed, he somehow becomes narcotized by what he sees.

The last step, according to Dr. Kline, is when the man begins to put it all into practice. He finally acts it out. Only a certain percentage will, but where do you think the sadists, the child abusers, the rapists come from? There is no such thing as a victimless crime. The porn addict is first of all a victim, but then later on he may seek his own victims. Pornography does not lead to degeneracy. It is degeneracy.

Pornography Is A Social Sickness

According to recent projections from statisticians, one out of every four baby girls born in the U.S. will be sexually molested by an adult male, many times a member of the same family. One out of every ten little baby boys will be sexually molested before puberty by an adult male. A former Harvard professor wrote a book in which he viewed Americans as victims of a sex mania as malignant as cancer and as socially menacing as communism.

There is a move to rid our society of "kiddie porn" magazines and materials which victimize innocent children and sometimes even babies. Many of these sick materials teach that women and children secretly desire sex, and to seduce them or even to rape them is to do them a favor. These warped materials suggest that when the victim resists by fighting and screaming, their paroxysms are responses of pleasure and that before long they will become passionate and willing lovers. Billions of dollars worth of this sewage is being spewed out all across America.

There are those who will claim that we need pornography, that it is a legitimate outlet that will heal a person by allowing him to express himself. If you believe that I would like to sell you the Hope Diamond.

No, pornography is not a legitimate outlet any more than alcohol is a good avenue for the alcoholic. You cannot cure an alcoholic by giving him alcohol. Neither do you heal a drug addict by making drugs available to him. And you certainly will not cure a sex pervert by handing him pornography. Anyone who believes that would try to put out a fire with gasoline.

A leading law official commented, "Not everyone who reads pornography is a sexual deviant, but all sex deviants read it." Herbert Chase, former Detroit police inspector, reported, "There has not been a sex murder in the history of our department in which the killer was not an avid reader of lewd magazines." They go together, accompanying each other.

Pornography Is A Domestic Disaster

Those who have counseled as I have can testify to the heartbreak and tragedy that have come into homes by husbands, who through reading and looking at this distortion of sex, have had their entire outlook on love, marriage, and sex so completely corrupted and twisted that a happy, tranquil, God-given love life is no longer possible, unless God does a radical cleansing of the mind.

The devil is uncannily clever. He realizes that if he can change what you think, he can change how you behave. That is why he is channeling sex right into your TV and your computer. It used to be a person had to sneak off to a dingy, sleazy "adult" movie house or to an "adult" shop to view pornographic films or videos. Now several cable TV networks and Internet sites can usher pornography into the inner sanctum of your home.

When the Playboy Channel came to Memphis, I clipped an article out of my local newspaper, *The Commercial Appeal:* "Playboy Channel Bringing Sex Unbridled Onto Home Screens. The Playboy organization is ready to bring raw sex, the kind of films that are seen in adult movie houses, right into the living rooms of the homes of Memphis." The writer, Brown Burnette, concluded by saying: "But the main significance of the rise of the Playboy Channel is the fact that one of the great taboos of the airwaves has been lifted. When you can watch sex on television in your home and hear those outlawed words spoken without the slightest trace of embarrassment, for better, for worse, a new day has dawned."[3]

A new day has not dawned. Rather, the sun has almost set. It is not a new day; it is the end of an age and the beginning of the judgment of God. My heart is broken, not because I am envious of the Playboy empire, but because I love families—boys and girls, husbands and wives.

Pornography Is Spiritual Suicide

Pornography, whether read, watched, or put into practice, is also spiritual suicide. Jesus taught, "But I say unto you that whoever looks at a woman to lust after her has already committed adultery with her in her heart" (Matthew 5:28). You cannot blame that statement on a backwoods preacher. It is the proclamation of the Lord Jesus Christ as

3. Brown Burnette, "Playboy Channel Bringing Sex Unbridled Onto Home Screens," *Commercial Appeal*, March 24, 1984, section C, p. 9.

He cries out, warning that one of these days the warm flames of lust will blaze up into the fiery holocaust of hell.

James perceptively analyzed the course and curse of lustful sin: "Then, when desire has conceived, it gives birth to sin, and sin, when it is full grown, brings forth death" (James 1:15).

This is the devil's LSD: lust-sin-death. Satan realizes if he can entice a person to lust, he can lure them deeper into sin. And when he snares a person deeply into sin, he has them.

You must think pure, holy, righteous, and good thoughts based on the Word of God. Romans 12:21 advises, "Do not overcome by evil, but overcome evil with good."

The secret to the mastery of the thought life is found in the verses of Proverbs that immediately precede Solomon's warning to keep your heart with all diligence. "My son, give attention to My words; incline your ear to My sayings. Do not let them depart from your eyes; keep them in the midst of your heart; for they are life to those who find them, and health to all their flesh" (Proverbs 4:20-22).

In other words, keep the Word of God in the midst of your heart. In order for you not to think bad thoughts, you must think God's thoughts. To keep from thinking negatively, you must think positively. Not only read the Word of God but study it. "Chew" on it. Absorb it. Let it sink down deeply into your heart and mind. Allow the principles of His Word to control you and dominate you. Genuine meditation, as I have written here, is thinking God's thoughts after Him. It is loading up on His Word.

This is why it is imperative that you have a quiet time every day, especially in the morning if possible. Do you? Do you arise in time to be alone with the Word of God? You must fellowship with Jesus, saturate your soul with the Word of God, and bathe yourself in the presence of God's dear Holy Spirit. That must become your lifestyle before the Lord.

Let me share a fantastic, profound concept with you. *God made you where you cannot think two things at the same time.* Consciously try to think more than one thought at a time. You can't do it, can you? It is not only "one step at a time, sweet Jesus," but also "one thought at a time, sweet Jesus." If you are thinking what is right, you cannot simultaneously be thinking what is wrong. My friend, it is that plainly simple and uncomplicated. You can choose your thoughts like your friends. That is why Paul wrote:

Finally, brethren, whatever things are true, whatever things are noble, whatever things are just, whatever things are pure, whatever things are lovely, whatever things are of good report, if there is any virtue and if there is anything praiseworthy-meditate on these things. (Philippians 4:8)

David posed this: "How can a young man cleanse his way? By taking heed according to Your Word... Your Word I have hidden in my heart, that I might not sin against You" (Psalm 119:9, 11).

When you begin to pack in the Word of God, you will discover that positive thoughts can also be powerful thoughts. Those thoughts will color and flavor all you do. By positive thoughts I am not referring to twittering birds, buzzing bees, the smell of flowers, or the rustle of the breeze in the trees, although those are invigorating. I have in mind the mighty Word of God.

Those Spirit-directed thoughts will cause you to become more and more like your Master, the Lord Jesus. "For the Word of God is living and powerful, and sharper than any two-edged sword..." (Hebrews 4:12a). The Word is powerful, decisive, and definitive.

Program the Word of God into your heart. Read it. Memorize it. Listen to it. Think of the time you spend driving to and from work. While others are honking and cursing and giving obscene gestures, why not drive and listen to the Word on tape? The truths of God's Word are powerful to cleanse and to keep.

THE MINISTRY OF THE THOUGHT LIFE

God desires to minister *to* you and *through* you in your thought life. When your thought life is right, there are at least three things it will begin to do for you. All three are found in Proverbs 4:23-27.

It Will Govern Your Speech.

"Put away from you a deceitful mouth, and put perverse lips far from you" (v. 24). It is a psychologically proven truth that your thought life will govern your speech. Listen to a person and find the wellsprings of his life. "Out of the heart proceed the issues of life" (see Matthew 15:18-19).

Do you stop and listen to people? As one has said, "They are frequently overheard saying nothing." Many of them are saying nothing, but others are belching up filth. Profane words reveal a profane heart. Dirty mouth—dirty heart. As they say in the country, "What's down in the well will come up in the bucket." Jesus reminds us, "...for out of the abundance of the heart the mouth speaks" (Matthew 12:34b).

It Will Guard Your Sight

Proverbs 4:25 says, "Let your eyes look straight ahead, and your eyelids look right before you." Have you ever had to look straight and neither to the left nor to the right? If you have walked past many newsstands, you understand what I mean. In such a case, you say to yourself, "Eyes, just keep looking straight ahead."

What you see governs how you think, right? Now, let's turn it around. How you think also governs what you see. Why do some people feast on lascivious, lewd things and others do not? Why do some people drink in pornography while others do not? It is because people have an ability to make up their minds whether they will or will not read or look at certain kinds of material. You are not merely a helpless victim. I am dead set against any form of pornography. No one is forcing you to buy it, rent it, read it, or watch it.

"I have made a covenant with my eyes; why then should I look upon a young woman?" (Job 31:1). Job, a righteous man, was exceedingly wise. He made a decision, and you ought to do the same. Determine that you will not allow a crack in the wall of your mind. You will keep your thought life with all diligence. You will answer no to the lust of the flesh and to the lust of the eyes and to the pride of life.

Do not put off your resolve until temptation is breathing down your neck. Make a covenant with your eyes beforehand, because, not only does what you see determine what you think, but what you think also determines what you see.

It Will Guide Your Steps

"Ponder the path of your feet, and let all your ways be established. Do not turn to the right or to the left: remove your foot from evil" (Proverbs 4:26-27). How can you do the will of God? Make sure you are thinking Christ's thoughts after Him. Be transformed by the renewing of your mind through the Holy Spirit and the Word of

God. Let the Spirit control your thought life. Then you can follow the will of God which He has for you.

God has a breathtakingly exciting life for you. He wants you to have His health, His wealth, and His wisdom. He wants you to enjoy the bonds of holy matrimony. He desires for you to have answered prayer. He wants you to know success to the fullest, highest meaning of the word.

But how are you going to do it? You will never experience a fulfilled life as a believer until you allow the Lord Jesus to dominate your thought life. Then God will guide your steps.

He understands what you are facing. Your best earthly friend can never care and understand and feel with you as much as Jesus does. Jesus is aware of everything that concerns you. In Him you have a never-ending relationship. "Casting all your care upon Him, for He cares for you" (1 Peter 5:7).

That is the wonderful ministry of the mind. It will govern your speech, guard your eyes, and guide your steps. "As a man thinketh... so is he!"

CHAPTER SIX

THE PLAYBOY'S PAYDAY

He shall die for lack of instruction; and in the greatness of his folly, he shall go astray. (Proverbs 5:23)

I began my romantic endeavors at a very young age. In school I fell in love with a little girl named Joyce, and my childhood sweetheart is now the love of my life.

It is different when you start young. I remember our first kiss. Chills ran up and down my spine... her Popsicle was melting!

Love and romance are wonderful. They are of universal interest. No matter who you are or where you live, you never really outgrow it.

It is true the girls mature and become interested a little bit before the boys. Up until age twelve the girls think about the boys before the boys start thinking about the girls. But from twelve to fourteen the boys are catching up with the girls; and from fourteen on they are on even footing.

Because love is so wonderful we need to find out what God thinks about it. Never have the idea that God is some sort of a cosmic killjoy. When God says, "Flee fornication," and, "Thou shalt not commit adultery," He is not trying to keep sex from us. He is trying to keep sex for us. It is His gift.

We should keep this in mind as we look into this fifth chapter of Proverbs.

THE DISCRETION WE SHOULD FOLLOW

My son, pay attention to My wisdom; lend your ear to My understanding, that you may preserve discretion, and your lips may keep knowledge. (Proverbs 5:1-2)

How are we going to learn what is right and what is wrong about sex? Are we going to learn it from Hollywood? Are we going to learn it from television? Are we going to learn it from the likes of Hugh Hefner, Dr. Ruth, and Jay Leno? Shall they be our teachers?

Hugh Hefner allegedly commented, "If Christ were here today and had to choose between being on the staff of *Playboy* magazine or being on the staff of one of the joy-killing, pleasure-denying churches, He would, of course, join us." The tragic thought is that Hugh Hefner does not know the "joy unspeakable and full of glory" that Jesus alone can give.

Youth need some answers. And parents are failing to give them. A Kansas State University study revealed that the parents of today's college women give them hardly any sex education. The major sources of such information, according to 110 female students, were friends, the media, and school courses.

Researcher Betsy Bergen reported the findings to the Society for the Scientific Study of Sex in St. Louis. "For these girls, you can probably sum up the impact that family has on sexuality in two words—not much," Bergen stated.

About 22 percent of the women said they were influenced to some extent in attitudes and values by parents. Twenty-eight percent said their attitudes about sex were similar to those held by their mothers. The college women were asked where they learned 35 items of sexual information. Mothers were the source for only two—fathers none!

Their feelings about sex before marriage were almost the reverse of their mothers' feelings. Sixty-six percent believed in sex before marriage if there was "affection between the couple." Only 23 percent believed in abstinence before marriage.

Sixty-seven percent of the mothers do not believe in having sex before marriage. Only 26 percent indicated they felt sex was all right before marriage.

This year the average American teenager will watch 2,500 hours of television. He will be assaulted by an endless array of scenes depicting or suggesting sexual intercourse. Four out of five of those scenes will involve characters who are not married to each other.

So where are we going to hear the truth? Are we going to receive the truth from the muck merchants and the dirt peddlers? Or are we going to get it from the God of glory who made us male and female in the beginning, and has watched over every marriage relationship and every sexual encounter from history until the present time? Personally, I choose the Word of God.

THE DECEPTION WE SHOULD AVOID

> For the lips of an immoral woman drip honey, and her mouth is smoother than oil: but in the end she is bitter as wormwood, sharp as a two-edged sword. Her feet go down to death, her steps lay hold of hell. Lest you ponder her path of life- her ways are unstable, you do not know them. (Proverbs 5:3-6)

While God gives discretion, the devil correspondingly gives deception. This strange woman, this prostitute, has lips that drip as a honey. I call her "old honey lips." She, at first, seems very enticing to this young man who is the king's son.

But Solomon gives his son some good, fatherly advice. It is, "Look out for old honey lips." Not only are her kisses sweet, but she is a real talker. Her lips are smoother than oil. Solomon is saying, "You had better look before you leap."

While working my way through school I was employed as an assistant to an elevator mechanic. The man I helped walked with a limp. My curiosity got the best of me, and I asked him what happened to his leg. He said, "You would hardly believe it if I told you, but I was working on an elevator several stories from the bottom. I sat on the floor and lifted the elevator so I could look beneath it. Then I remembered some tools I had left in the pit. I grabbed the bottom of that elevator, swung under, and let go. I'd forgotten that I'd run the elevator up a number of floors."

You remark, "How foolish." That's right, you are supposed to look before you leap. That is exactly Solomon's point. This impure woman has three major weapons in her arsenal:

Emotional Involvement

For the commandment is a lamp, and the law is light; reproofs of instruction are the way of life, to keep you from the evil woman, from the flattering tongue of the seductress. (Proverbs 6:23-24)

She is skilled at flattery and uses it as one of her chief weapons. Someone has said, "Flattery is like perfume. It's all right to sniff it, but you are not supposed to swallow it."

She says, "You're so handsome; you're so strong; you're so wise; you're so kind. I need you. I just think you're a wonderful man." Flattery makes big fools of little men.

Beware of emotional involvement that is not rooted in trust and sincerity. Sexual sin is often the end result of carnal conversation. Notice that "the commandment is a lamp, and the law is light..." (Proverbs 6:23a) to keep the young man pure.

The basis of a happy date life that leads to a godly home life is the Word of God. The early attraction between a man and a woman should be spiritual, not emotional.

Physical Allurement

Do not lust after her beauty in your heart. (Proverbs 6:25a)

She may be a candidate for a centerfold and you think, *Boy, that is for me.* But the Bible counters, "Charm is deceitful and beauty is passing, but a woman who fears the LORD, she shall be praised" (Proverbs 31:30b).

Of course, there is nothing wrong with a woman being beautiful. Physical beauty is a gift from God. I want to remind the girls, however: what you are depending on to catch a man with, is what you are going to have to keep him with. And if he loves you because of your beauty, what are you going to do when your beauty is no longer there?

A weird poet wrote, "Beauty is skin deep, but ugly goes all the way to the bone. Beauty fades, but ugly holds its own." It is passing.

It can be vain. But a woman who fears the Lord becomes more and more beautiful every day.

That's the reason the apostle Peter wrote, "Do not let your adornment be merely outward – arranging the hair, wearing of gold, or of putting on fine apparel - rather let it be the hidden person of the heart, with the corruptible beauty of a gentle and quiet spirit, which is in very precious in the sight of God " (1 Peter 3:3-4).

Godly beauty is incorruptible. That is, it is not going to fade, it is not going to decay. I still think you ought to be as physically beautiful as possible. Sometimes someone will ask if I think it is a sin for a woman to wear makeup. I think it is a sin if some women *don't* wear makeup!

You are not going to win a husband by looking like something left over from a rummage sale. Yet, a lasting relationship cannot be built on something as fading as physical beauty.

Sexual Enticement

Neither let her allure you with her eyelids. (Proverbs 6:25b)

This woman bats those big eyelashes at him, winks, and gives that "come-hither look." That's what happens in these singles bars. They'll sit there, and then after a while she'll look at him without having to speak a word. He looks back at her, and the poor sucker is gone. She has taken him "with her eyelids" because she knows how to flirt.

The sad fact is that many times she doesn't really want him. She just wants what he has. While she is stroking his hair, she is really after his scalp. Beware of the deception.

And it also works the other way around. A man will carry a woman out and wine and dine her. He'll begin to pour the sugar in her ear and murmur, "I love you, I really love you." Then he'll ask her, "Do you really love me?" If she answers "yes" then he'll demand, "Prove it."

Sexual immorality never proves love. Love is proven when you can appreciate and enjoy a person and their character without having to sully their purity to do it.

The Bible presents this picture of unfeigned love: "And Jacob served seven years for Rachel; and they seemed unto him but a few days, for the love he had to her" (Genesis 29:20). Even though he was tricked and conned by his father-in-law, Laban, Jacob was willing to labor and wait for Rachel, his true love.

You see, lust can't wait. But love can wait. So when that guy sighs, "I love you, baby. I love you. I love you." what he really means is, "I love *me*. I love *me*. I love *me*. I want my own selfish, carnal wishes. I want to please me. I don't care about your welfare. I'm in love with me."

A man will go out into an orange grove, pick one of those big, succulent oranges, take his penknife, cut a plug out of it, put it up to his mouth, and squeeze all of the juice out of it. Then he'll throw it on the ground like a piece of garbage, wipe his mouth, and say, "Man, I just love oranges." Young lady, that's how he loves you. And you are left like a piece of garbage.

Sexual enticement will never be the basis for a lasting and fulfilling relationship. Look before you leap.

THE DISTANCE WE SHOULD KEEP

> Therefore hear Me now, My children, and do not depart from the words of My mouth. Remove your way far from her, and do not do near the door of her house. (Proverbs 5:7-8)

The sin of immorality is not one we are instructed to fight. It is one we are told to flee! The Bible commands, "Flee fornication" and "Flee youthful lusts."

Run from that compromising situation. If someone who works in your office is flirting with you, and you feel that lust and that attraction, it would be better for you to quit than to stay in that office. You reply, "But my job!" I answer, "But your purity!"

Don't see how close you can come to the edge without falling over. See how far you can stay away. Flee fornication! I know what young men feel. I felt it. They claim that what a man thinks about he becomes. When I was in college, I almost turned into a girl! Man, it's real. But I had a motto on my desk: "He who would not fall down ought not to walk in slippery places."

Don't put garbage and filth into your mind. Don't go to those movies. Don't read those magazines. Don't watch that program. Don't do it!

"Can a man take fire into his bosom, and his clothes not be burned?" (Proverbs 6:27).

THE DAMAGE WE MAY SUFFER

Lest thou give your honor to others, and your years to the cruel one; lest aliens be filled with your wealth, and your labors go in the house of a foreigner. (Proverbs 5:9-10)

Dissipation

It costs to be a playboy. Sin will keep you from being prosperous and from having what God wants you to possess.

There was an eminently successful businessman at the top of his profession. He lived in one of the most beautiful homes and had one of the best businesses in the city. This man also had a loving wife and fantastic kids. He literally had it all.

Then a girl came along. What some would call a "harmless flirtation" began as the girl batted those false eyelashes at him and told him how wonderful he was. It seemed innocent to some at first, but she sank her hooks into him, and he didn't have enough sense to say no.

That thread of flirtation became a cord, and that cord became a cable, and that cable became a chain, and that man lost everything.

Now his little children call somebody else daddy and his wife is married to another man. Someone else is living in that beautiful home. Dissipation! Sin is a costly item.

Disease

And you mourn at last, when your flesh and your body are consumed. (Proverbs 5:11)

He is talking about the vile venereal diseases that can come through immorality. They are God's curse.

People used to fool themselves by alibiing, "If I get a disease, there is penicillin and sulfa. I can be cured of gonorrhea and syphilis in a short while and be at it again." But certain strains of venereal diseases are now resistant to drugs. Social diseases are on the rampage.

The Word speaks about people whose bodies are literally being eaten up and consumed. AIDS was virtually unknown until the early eighties. Now it is ravaging thousands of homosexuals, heterosexuals, bisexuals, and many others who are innocent of sexual sin. Babies and young children are contracting this unspeakably horrible disease. The extent and outreach of AIDS is epidemic and frightening.

Many promiscuous people from all walks of life are thinking twice about their partners. According to opinion polls across our country, many previously sexually active people are even totally abstaining from all sexual contact.

There is no known cure for AIDS. And other venereal diseases are difficult to cure, if at all. Another aspect of this problem is: the innocent often suffer because of the guilty. Multiplied babies and children have been damaged for life because of social diseases contracted from their parents or others. That is part and parcel of the playboy's payday. That is part of the so-called sexual revolution that has supposedly set us "free."

A strapping young man with broad shoulders, a square jaw, and a big grin was walking down the streets of Lubbock, Texas. He was out on a lark, on his way to a "big time." A crippled old man in a wheelchair called to him, "Son, I want to ask you a question. Are you good at mathematics?"

The young man replied, "Yes sir, I'm pretty good."

The old man said, "Then I have an equation for you. Fifteen minutes of pleasure with a girl down on the border and a lifetime being a cripple in a wheelchair—are they equal?"

The young man answered, "No sir, they aren't equal."

The crippled man said, "Then be sure your sins will find you out."

There are those who bristle at the idea of disease being judgment on our sin, yet we have no trouble accepting the fact that our automobiles will self-destruct if we drive them without oil. C. S. Lewis reminds us, "Moral rules are directions for running the human machine. Every moral rule is to prevent a breakdown, or a strain, or a friction, in the running of that machine."

Disappointment

And say, 'How have I hated instruction, and my heart despised correction! I have not obeyed the voice of my teachers, nor inclined my ear to those who instructed me! (Proverbs 5:12-13)

These verses say, "Why wouldn't I listen to God's Word? Why wouldn't I listen to the Holy Spirit? Why wouldn't I listen to my mother and father? Why wouldn't I listen to my pastor? Why did I think I was so smart?"

Sin offers much, but it pays little. You cannot beat the system. And one of these days you are going to reach a time of dismal disappointment. Unless you heed God's Word, when you come to the end of it all, you will have missed the best of life.

Hugh Hefner, the *Playboy* king, presumably can have all the sensual pleasure he wants. He is reported to have said on one occasion, "In the next ten years I would rather meet a girl and fall in love and have her fall in love with me than to make another $100 million dollars."

What he is saying is, "I've got it all, but I don't have satisfaction. There is something that is worth more than $100 million dollars to me, and I don't have it."

Marilyn Monroe, the goddess of sex and pleasure, said, "I hate sex." And eventually she committed suicide. Sweden, supposedly one of the most liberated countries in the world with open pornography, open prostitution, and "free love," has the highest divorce rate of any nation. "God is not mocked" (Galatians 6:7b). The cup of sin is sweet, but the dregs are bitter indeed.

An in-depth study at Stanford University concluded that the more promiscuous people were before marriage, the less chance for happiness after marriage. This idea of "try before you buy" may sound cute, but it is not in the Word of God.

Young people today think there is absolutely nothing wrong with meeting someone and jumping into bed with them. But a head psychologist in one of America's major universities reported "More than 50 percent of the students on this campus have psychological problems because of their immoral relationships."

The American sexual revolution that was supposed to lead to sexual utopia has run into serious trouble. *Time* magazine ran a cover story, announcing: "The (Sexual) Revolution Is Over."

A former advocate of the "new morality" has written, "The sexual revolution, in slaying some loathsome old dragons, has created some formidable new ones."

We should not be surprised at the disappointment. Solomon warned us long ago.

Disgrace

> I was on the verge of total ruin, in the midst of the assembly and congregation. (Proverbs 5:14)

The Living Bible says, "For now I must face public disgrace."

Nowadays public disgrace means little to some people. I read where a woman was put out of a church and publicly censured because she was living in immorality. She was not humiliated. She turned around and sued the church for defamation of character. Vance Havner has well said, "Sin that used to slink down the back alleys now struts down Main Street."

Yet, one of these days at the judgment, dear friend, that which is done in secret will be shouted from the rooftops. Your mother will know, your spouse will know, your pastor will know, your children will know. Disgrace is part of the playboy's payday. Sooner or later it will come.

Dominion

> His own iniquities entrap the wicked man, and he is caught in the cords of his sin. (Proverbs 5:22)

The Tyrant of Syracuse called the blacksmith before the throne. This despot instructed the blacksmith, "I want to see you make a chain." And so the blacksmith got his bellows, his forge, his hammer, his anvil, and his molten metal, and began to forge a chain.

When he finished he held the chain up to the Tyrant of Syracuse and boasted, "There, sire, is an example of my work. That chain is so strong and so powerful, that you could put a team of horses on either end, and they would not be able to part it asunder."

Then with a cruel sneer, the Tyrant commanded, "Guards, seize the blacksmith, chain him with that chain, and cast him into the dungeon."

There is another more cruel than the Tyrant of Syracuse, and he is the devil. But the devil can only chain us with the cold steel chains we ourselves have forged!

I am thinking of a young man. He was one of the finest young men I've ever met. He hailed from one of the best families I've ever known. He married an indescribably lovely girl, but somehow he became enamored with a young lady with whom he was working. One thing led to another until they were living in adultery and sin.

I persuaded him to come and talk with me. We sat in my study. I opened God's Word and read it to him. Then, I asked him, "Son, do you believe the Bible is the Word of God?"

"Yes sir."

"Do you believe God loves you?"

"Yes sir."

"Do you believe God's laws are for your welfare and for your good?"

"Yes sir."

"Do you believe God will forgive you if you'll repent?"

"Yes sir."

"Son, are you willing to repudiate this thing, to repent, and put it under the blood of Jesus? Will you get on your knees with me right now and ask God to cleanse you and to give you a new start?"

"Yes, Pastor, I will."

I said, "Oh, thank you, Jesus."

We fell on our knees, and I wept and prayed. He wept and prayed. I said, "Now that you've asked God to forgive you, are you willing to go to your wife and ask her to forgive you and put your home back together? Will you let your children have a Christian daddy, someone they can look up to?"

"Yes sir, I am. Thank you, Pastor, for helping me."

He walked out with a big smile on his face. I prayed, "Thank you, Jesus, for another victory." But in three or four weeks, that young man was back with that other woman, back in sin, back in disgrace, back in heartbreak.

The home is now irrevocably broken. And my heart is broken. I believe that this young man, sincere as he was, failed to understand the strength of this sin.

People talk about "free love." These people are not free. They are slaves to lust. Jesus can make that young man free. What I told him would have worked if he had followed through.

I can show you case after case of people who have gone the same route and have found victory and deliverance. But I am saying it requires a supernatural working of God to break the shackles of sin.

Praise God, the Bible says to the Christian, sin shall no longer have dominion over you (see Romans 6:14).

Death

> He shall die for lack of instruction, and in the greatness of his folly he shall go astray. (Proverbs 5:23)

To die without instruction is to die in sin. It is to die and go to hell. I must emphasize this. There are a lot of carnal church members who are living double lives and feeling smug because their names are on the church roll. They are living in open, flagrant immorality and somehow have the idea that God is going to overlook it.

The Bible says, "Be not deceived: neither fornicators, nor idolaters, nor adulterers, nor effeminate, nor abusers of themselves with mankind...shall inherit the kingdom of God" (1 Corinthians 6:9b,10b). If you are unrepentantly living this kind of a lifestyle, the Bible indicates you are lost and going to hell.

Don't get the idea that Jesus died to save you from hell. He didn't die to save you *from hell,* He died to save you *from sin.* Being saved from hell is simply the result of being saved from sin.

Does that mean if you've done any of these things you can't be saved? No, Paul continues in 1 Corinthians 6, "And such were some of you, But you were washed" (v. 11a). You are sanctified, you are justified—hallelujah, Amen!

There is no sin He cannot forgive unless a person has crossed the deadline and willfully shut his heart in God's face. Not a blot, not a blemish, not a stain He cannot forgive. The blood of Jesus Christ, God's Son, makes the vilest sinner clean. "If we confess our sins, He is faithful and just to forgive us our sins and to cleanse us from all unrighteousness" (1 John 1:9).

You may be saved right now and living in sin. If you are, God is already chastising you, or preparing to do so. If you are living in immorality, I can say without fear of contradiction that you are either headed for the woodshed or you are headed for hell. For you to go on in that kind of a continuing relationship is a sign that you do not know the God of grace, the God of glory.

"Therefore, if any man be in Christ, he is a new creation" (2 Corinthians 5:17a). Eternal punishment in hell is the ultimate playboy's payday. This message must be heard across America.

Kids talk about "going all the way" in sexual relationships. Young person, you have not gone all the way until you stand before God in judgment.

You are free to choose, but you are not free to choose the consequences of your choices. You do not so much break God's laws as you are broken on them.

THE DESIGN WE SHOULD FOLLOW

God's design is without flaw. It will work. God created male and female. He saw that it was good. He performed the first wedding ceremony in the Garden of Eden. I like that old song, "One man, one wife, one love through life. Memories are made of this." First, God intends for...

A Legal Marriage

Drink water from your own cistern, and running water from your own well. (Proverbs 5:15)

What does that mean? That a man ought not to drink or use water from another man's source. It carries over into your life. Settle down with one woman, with one man. Establish a home. God did not merely intend for you to "live together."

It is estimated that three or four million American men and women are living together without a legal ceremony. When I was a boy that was called "shacking up." Only the lowliest people lived like that in those days. Now it has become all the rage. One silly woman chirped, "I don't want to get married because I'm afraid I'll get divorced." Ridiculous.

God's plan is "one man, one wife, one love through life." Settle down with one wife and be faithful to her. One husband and be faithful to him. "Therefore a man shall leave his father and mother and be joined to his wife, and they shall become one flesh" (Genesis 2:24). One in body, mind, and soul.

God never intended divorce. Jesus explained that God reluctantly allowed it because of the hardness of men's hearts. Work at your marriage if God honors you with a mate. It is strange that many people will spend more time washing their cars or balancing their checkbooks than maintaining their marriages. In the sight of

God a marriage is indissoluble. A divorce, a breakup does violence to His divine plan.

An anonymous poet penned these lines:

HOME IS...

Where joy is shared,
And sorrow eased,
Where fathers and mothers
Are respected and loved,
Where children are wanted.
Where the simplest food
Is good enough for kings
Because it is earned.
Where money is not so important
As loving kindness;
Where even the teakettle
Sings for happiness.

Second, God intends for...

A Loving Mate

> Let your fountain be blessed, and rejoice with the wife of your youth. As a loving deer and a graceful doe, let her breasts satisfy you at all times; and always be enraptured with her love. (Proverbs 5:18-19)

The *Playboy* philosophy has fostered the mistaken notion that God is against sex. The fact is God created sex. It was He who instructed Adam and Eve to "be fruitful and multiply and fill the earth." God is the Creator of sex.

The Heavenly Father knows what is best since He gave sex to us. That is why He teaches us to leave our parents and to cleave to our mate. Sex is a fearfully sacred function, ordained of God. Latent within sex is the possibility of a new life, a person for whom Christ died.

God wants you to be fulfilled. He understands your so-called urges and drives since He placed them there, but with the understanding that He would control them as you yield yourself to Him. He wants you to have sexual fulfillment in marriage.

God wants you to have real joy. And my heart is crushed because I am afraid that many young people are going to miss God's best.

Several years ago *Redbook* magazine questioned 100,000 women about their sex lives. It was the most extensive survey of female sexuality since Kinsey's studies. The most astonishing finding was the discovery of a direct link between sexual satisfaction and religious commitment. The survey showed that no matter what the age, education, or income of respondents, women who described themselves as "strongly religious" were far more likely to describe their sex lives as highly satisfying than were their nonreligious counterparts.

When God says, "Thou shalt not," He is actually saying, "Don't hurt yourself. I am trying to protect you." He is inviting, "Help yourself to happiness." I would not trade my Christian home for anything in this world. I am grateful my wife and I were pure when we came to the marriage altar. I praise God for the sweet, pure Christian girl I married. Every day I praise God for the joy He has given me in my family with my wife and with our children.

If you eat your cake today, you'll have a crumby tomorrow! Amen! If you are not saved, I cannot imagine how you are going to make it in this sex-saturated society. If you are saved, you ought to pray to be filled with the Holy Spirit. You see, you can be saved and still backslide and disappoint your Lord. I have seen many a Christian put Jesus to an open shame because they took Christ off the throne and walked in the flesh.

If you are not married, you should pray and seek God's guidance. It is estimated that 90 percent of all singles want to find a mate. Perhaps God intends for some to remain single. Each person must decide that within his/her own heart under the leadership of the Holy Spirit. Under most circumstances, God wants you to have a mate.

You ask, "But how can I find that person? I have looked and looked and looked." To find the right person you must be the right person. Dedicate yourself. "Lord, I want to be that right person someone is looking for and praying for right now."

If you are the right person you are not going to find "Mr. Right" or "Mrs. Right" in a singles' bar or a nightclub. You need to seek out a born-again partner in a Christian environment. There are more decent people out there than you realize. Pray that God will lead you to the right person, and make sure you yourself are right.

If you have sinned, confess it and repent of it. If you've been divorced and remarried, take what you do have and give it to Jesus. You can't unscramble eggs. Put it under the blood of Jesus Christ. Start now to build a Christian home. Christ will cleanse and forgive you.

Amid this playboy society, God has a wonderful, fulfilling plan for your life. I pray you will not let it pass you by!

CHAPTER SEVEN

THE FRIENDSHIP FACTOR

A friend loves at all times, and a brother is born for adversity. (Proverbs 17:17)

One of the basic needs and longings of our hearts is for a real friend, a true friend. Many people have given definitions of this type of friend. Erma Bombeck remarked, "A friend is somebody who doesn't go on a diet when you're fat."

Others have commented, "A friend is someone who knows all about you and loves you just the same." Or, "A true friend will go on liking you, no matter how successful either of you becomes."

On a more serious note it has been said, "A friend is one who strengthens you with his prayers, blesses you with his love, and encourages you with his hope." Or, "A friend is one to whom distance is no barrier to communication, to concern, or to caring." Or, "A friend is someone who believes in you when you have ceased to believe in yourself." Or, "A friend is somebody who is on the scene when you need him and quietly leaves when you want to be left alone." And another put it like this, "A friend is someone who is there when you call and sometimes even before you call."

All of these are splendid thoughts and opinions. But what does the Bible have to say about this matter of friendship? Because, you see, the Bible places a heavy emphasis on friends.

THE VALUE OF FRIENDSHIP

A friend loves at all times. (Proverbs 17:17a)

A true friend is of infinite value, and I do not have many true friends. That might seem rather strange to you. You might think I ought to be overrun with friends. Now I do have plenty of wonderful acquaintances. I enjoy them, and I thank God for them. But a true friend is a rare find.

I used to hear people say, "If you can count your friends on one hand you're fortunate." And I would think, *Not me. I've got a lot of friends. All the guys I played football with, my classmates, the folks I know at church. Why, I have hundreds of friends.*

But the older I become, and hopefully the wiser I grow, the more I understand what people mean when they talk about the rarity of a true friend.

We all touch people on different levels. Our lives are like an ocean vessel on a journey through the sea of life. There are many people who just hop on and off board. These are the casual acquaintances we meet. They touch our lives briefly, we enjoy them, we learn from them, but then they are gone.

Then there are other friends. I would call them fair-weather friends. They climb on board and sail for a while, but when a storm comes they abandon ship.

Thank God there is a third kind of friend—a true friend, a real friend. When they board, they stay aboard. In the calm they are there; in the storm they are there. When the wind is whipping they are there; when the lightning is flashing they are there. And they will not leave until they see you safely into port.

That is the kind of friend I have in mind. And I do not have many of these true, genuine friends. Nor do you. And as a matter of fact, the Bible warns us against having too many friends. Proverbs 18:24a, in the *New American Standard Bible*, translates, "A man of too many friends comes to ruin."

That is an amazing verse. What is the reason behind it? I believe it is because friends are costly to have. It requires effort. It takes time.

A real friend is someone in whom you are going to invest your energy, your prayers, your time. A genuine friendship will be a demand upon your social life, your financial life, and your emotional life. And you cannot afford the luxury of many friends because it would be impossible to maintain them. You need only one mate and only a few friends.

When I was in seminary the professors used to tell us a pastor ought not to have any personal friends on his church field. It would make the other people jealous and envious. And the pastor's wife should not have any friends. I believe that is bad advice. To counsel anyone who lives that they should not have friends is to deny their basic humanity.

Even the Lord Jesus Christ, when He was here in the flesh, had His friends. He loved everybody, but He had His friends. There were twelve disciples, but out of those twelve there was that inner trinity of disciples—Peter, James, and John—who were more intimate. And out of Peter, James, and John there was one, John, who was the "beloved" disciple.

Jesus loved many people, but there was one home where He would often stay. It was the home of Mary, Martha, and Lazarus. These were His special friends. They were the ones who ministered to Him. And if the Lord Jesus, in His humanity, needed a friend, so must you. Remember, do not have too many. But you must have some. Ben Franklin, a very wise man, counseled, "Be slow in making your friends—even slower in changing them."

THE VIRTUES OF FRIENDSHIP

There are no bargain friendships. They are certainly costly, but I want you to understand why they are worth the investment.

True Friendship Is Selfless

A friend loves at all times. (Proverbs 17:17a)

Certain people will claim to be your friend, and yet they will attach certain conditions upon their friendship. They will stipulate, "I love you if," or, "I love you when," or, "I will love you until," or, "I love you because."

That is, if I can satisfy their needs they will be my friend. But it will not be a true friendship, because when the "if," the "when," the "until," or the "because" is not exactly right, overboard they will go.

A real friend is a selfless one who loves you, not because of any need in himself as such. A true friend is one who possesses an unconditional love that proves, "I love you—period."

True Friendship Is Steadfast

A friend loveth at all times. (Proverbs 17:17a)

An English publication had a contest for the best definition of a friend. Some of the ones that won honorable mentions were: "A friend is somebody who multiplies your joys and divides your griefs;" "A friend is someone who understands your silence."

But let me give you the one which won the prize. "A real friend is someone who comes in when the whole world has gone out." That is another means of saying, "A friend loves at all times."

Do you want to find out who your friends are? Then make a mistake—not a little one, but make a big one, and see what happens. Most of those people you thought were your friends will desert you like rats leaving a sinking ship. They were not true friends. Proverbs 27:10a says, "Do not forsake your own friend or your father's friend." It does not matter what you have done, a true-blue friend is still going to be there.

I like this little poem by an unknown author:

Don't walk in front of me—
    I may not follow:
Don't walk behind me—
    I may not lead.
Walk beside me—
    And just be my friend.

True Friendship Is Sacrificial

But there is a friend that sticks closer than a brother. (Proverbs 18:24b)

Sometimes it would be easier to forsake your friend than to become involved in his trouble. Yes, friendship is costly. The Indians have a word for *friend*. Translated into English it means, "One who carries my sorrows on his back."

That reminds me of the Lord Jesus. "Surely He has borne our griefs and carried our sorrows" (Isaiah 53:4). "What a friend we have in Jesus!" It cost the Lord Jesus to wear the title, *A Friend of Sinners*. "Greater love has no one than this, than to lay down one's life for his friends" (John 15:13).

True Friendship Is Sanctifying

> As iron sharpens iron, so a man sharpens the countenance of his friend. (Proverbs 27:17)

You do not sharpen an ax on a pound of butter. And if you have a real friend, he is going to have an uplifting, sharpening influence on your life. He is going to make you a better person. He will put the cutting edge on your life.

A false friend will blunt your influence; a false friend will dull your usefulness; a false friend will wear you down.

And so one of the measurements as to whether or not that person is a real friend is this, "Am I a better person when I am in his presence?"

Now while it is true that a genuine friend will never forsake you, it is equally true that a real friend will never condone your wrongdoing. He will always confront you that he might change you. A true friend will smooth the rough edges off your life.

There is a bittersweet verse of Scripture found in Proverbs 27:6, "Faithful are the wounds of a friend, but the kisses of an enemy are deceitful." Judas kissed the Lord, but it was a kiss of deceit, a kiss of flattery. "Judas kissed the door to heaven and went to hell."

Flattery comes from false friends. A true friend may compliment you, but he will never flatter you, because under the skin hypocrisy and flattery are twins. The only difference is this: a hypocrite will say behind your back what he will not say to your face, while a flatterer will say to your face what he will not say behind your back. The two are brothers.

True friends love us enough to confront. In February 1979, about 10:30 on a Saturday evening I was sitting in my recliner looking over my sermon notes for the next day and preparing for bed. I started to get up and I felt a pain, mostly all over. I tried to figure it out but could not.

I thought, *I'll just take a couple of Alka Seltzers and go to bed. In the morning I'll be all right.* At one o'clock in the morning, I was still awake and could not get any relief. I stumbled around the house trying to find some sort of a medical book so I could do a bit of research. And I thought, *You know, this is silly. You might be having a heart attack, and you will just sit here and read while you die. You know Joyce would not like that.*

You ask, "Where was Joyce?" She was out of town. That was part of the problem. I had done my own cooking. Actually, for lunch I had eaten at a restaurant. I had a chili dog. And then for dinner I searched the cabinet until I found a can of hot tamales. I emptied them out, heated them in the microwave, bathed them with Tabasco sauce, wolfed them down, and ran out to a meeting. Obviously, that triggered something.

In I walked to the emergency room. I felt so silly going. But I sheepishly drove to that hospital and felt so weak when I finally surrendered. It was as if I was saying, "Here I am. I'm turning myself in."

I remember talking to that doctor. I poured it out, "Now, Doctor, it isn't my heart. I've got a good heart. And it isn't my appendix. The pain is on the wrong side. And it isn't the flu. I don't have a fever."

He interrupted, "Do you think you could be quiet for just a minute?" Then he did a few preliminary tests and said, "Have you ever thought about your gall bladder?" He made some pictures of me and found a rock collection down there.

And then my good friend, Dr. Dave Dunavant, came in and informed me, "Preacher, we are going to take that out." And guess what he did? I'm talking about a good friend now. He put me on a table, and he cut me. I mean, he sliced into me. He didn't shed a tear. It didn't bother him a bit. I think he rather enjoyed it. He cut me!

Why would one friend do that to another friend? "Faithful are the wounds of a friend" (Proverbs 27:6a). *He hurt me that he might heal me. He hurt me because he loved me.*

The test of a true friend is this: Are you a better person because of your friend? I am not with my true friends more than five minutes before they are giving me a new thought, a new blessing, a new idea. They are constantly adding to my life because they have riches from the Word of God to give me.

Someone wrote these heartfelt words, "I love you not for what you are, but for what I am when I am with you. I love you, not only for what you have made of yourself, but for what you are making of me. I love you for not closing your ears to the discord in me, but for adding to the music in me by worshipful listening. You have done it without a touch, without a word, without a sign. You have done it by just being yourself. Perhaps this is what being a friend means after all."

THE VENTURE OF FRIENDSHIP

There are certain spiritual and practical ways of entering into this venture of friendship. *Meet the best Friend whose name is Jesus.* He has all the attributes of a true friend. He is a selfless Friend Who first loved you (see 1 John 4:19). He is a steadfast Friend Who will never leave you nor forsake you (see Hebrews 13:5).

He is a sacrificial Friend for "Greater love has no man than this, than to lay down his life for one's friends" (John 15:13). He is a sanctifying Friend who can make you into the kind of a person He wants you to be (see Philippians 1:6).

Even His enemies called Him "a friend of sinners." And that He is. You see, He doesn't love us because we are lovely. He simply loves us. He doesn't love us because we are valuable. No, we are valuable *because* He loves us. He doesn't change you in order to love you. He loves you in order to change you. That's the kind of friend we have in the Lord Jesus Christ. "But God demonstrates His own love toward us, in that while we were still sinners, Christ died for us" (Romans 5:8).

And the reason that many of you do not have human friends is because you do not have Jesus as your closest Friend. Many people do not have friends because they are not the kind of persons with whom it is easy to be a friend. They have a basic character flaw that makes them obnoxious to be around.

The character flaw is insecurity, and this insecurity portrays itself and rears its ugly head in their lives as selfishness. An insecure person does not feel he has anything to give. Therefore he wants to constantly take, take, take. And the hidden reason behind their desire for friendship is to find someone else to latch onto and leech strength from. It is a "getting" relationship with nothing to give in return.

The solution is to meet the Lord Jesus Who knows all about you and loves you in spite of your weakness. This is grace—that God accepts you totally apart from what you have done. He accepts you as you are, "warts and all."

Faith is your acceptance of the fact that He accepts you. Now, repeat after me: *He accepts me. I accept that He accepts me. Now I can accept me. It is all right for me to love what Jesus loves. And if Jesus loves me, I can love me.*

Some people will piously pontificate that you are not supposed to love yourself. I wonder what they do with the verse where Jesus teaches that we are to love our neighbor as we love ourselves (see Matthew 22:39). If you do not love yourself, how are you going to love anybody else? You must have a basic self-love that is based on the fact that the Lord has made you "accepted in the Beloved" (Ephesians 1:6b).

When I declare that you are to love yourself, that does not mean you are to stand in front of the mirror and sing "How Great Thou Art." I am talking about the fact that in the Lord Jesus you are a somebody! You are a royal blueblood, a child of the King! That deals with your basic security.

Now stay with me here. *He accepts me; I accept the fact that He accepts me; I therefore accept me. Now I am free to accept you. I no longer have to be pumping you. I no longer have to manipulate you. I no longer have to use you. I can love you because of who you are, not because of what I need for you to give me. I can love you as a real person, and now you are free to love me because that ugliness has been removed.*

That is the basis of friendship, and it is found in the Lord Jesus Christ. When Jesus was here on earth He was only able to spend time with a few friends. And you are thinking, *I wish I could have been one of them.* An exciting verse is found in John 15:15 where Jesus says, "No longer do I call you servants, for the servant does not know what his master is doing; but I have called you friends, for all things that I heard from My Father I have made known to you."

In this passage of Scripture the Lord Jesus is preparing to return to His Father, and He asserts in John 16:7b, "It is to your advantage that I go away; for if I do not go away, the Helper will not come to you; but if I depart, I will send Him to you."

It is the Holy Spirit Who is the personal Friend to everyone who is a Christian. When Jesus was here in the flesh He could not spend the night in everybody's home. But now He spends the night in my home! He could not be intimate with everyone, but now He is intimate with me! And He can be intimate with you, as fully and intimately as if He had no other friend in the entire world! He does it through the Holy Spirit.

And when I know that Friend of friends, my needs are met with such sufficiency that I am free to love you without demands. And you are free to love me in return because of it.

Nelson L. Price suggests:

> For a gratifying life, spend it developing friendships in order to use them as a basis for sharing the summons of God. Remember these guidelines for establishing friendships:
>
> - *Consider good relationships a priority.* Many people fail to do this and live a lonely life. Friendships are self-rewarding. Emerson noted our displaced priorities and commented: "We take care of our health, we lay up money, we make our roof tight, and our clothing sufficient; but who provides wisely that he shall not be wanting in the best property of all—friends?" Christ is the prototype of making friends. He established caring relationships. He called persons friends. They sensed Him to be their confidante.
>
> - *Be open and share of yourself...* Don't wall yourself in. In doing so you wall others out. Many Christians can name only a few non-Christians among their friends. If the Christian world does not make friends with a purpose, who can give a loving encouragement to accept God's summons?
>
> - *Show your love...* Love melts frost from a frigid friendship. It thaws frozen relationships. Don't hesitate discreetly to use expressions of endearment. Express your regard for persons.
>
> - *Be attentive to others' expressions of friendship.* Don't overlook overtures by others that might open up a friendship. Be attentive to the gestures of kindness shown you. Respond sensitively.[4]

Take the initiative. "For whatever a man sows, that he will also reap" (Galatians 6:7b). If you want a friend, you must be a friend. You are going to get what you give. If you want love, that is what you are going to have to give. "Give, and it will be given to you" (Luke 6:38a). People who want to have friends must show themselves friendly.

---

4. Nelson L. Price, *Called To Splendor* (Nashville, TN: Broadman & Holman Publishers, 1984), pp.50-51.

There are multitudes of people out there who are waiting for someone to come and be their friend. "I went out to find a friend and did not find one there. I went out to be a friend and friends were everywhere." Dale Carnegie wrote, "You can make more friends in two months by becoming really interested in other people than you can in two years by trying to get other people interested in you."

Be practical. Put yourself into the type of place where the right kind of friends are. This is in a church, not a singles' bar. You will most likely meet true friends in the social context of Christian people. Be the right person in the right place.

Take risks. Break the ice. Find someone with a common interest and begin to share with that person. Of course there is a risk. You might be rejected or embarrassed, but you are able to risk it because Christ has already filled those emotional voids in your life.

Be yourself. Do not put on. Be your best self, but do not try to be what you are not.

Be reasonable. Do not try to make it happen overnight. There are no true "instant" friendships. Do not force it. Do not do an overkill. You may drive that new friend away. Let it happen. Trust God to grow the relationship. Never be guilty of pulling your radishes up by the roots to see how they are growing and then jamming them back into the ground.

Do not make unreasonable demands. Do not smother your new friend.

If you will follow this approach and pray, "God give me a friend," He will. "But my God shall supply all your need according to His riches in glory by Christ Jesus" (Philippians 4:19). God answers prayer, and He will send you a friend.

CHAPTER EIGHT

GOD'S ANSWER TO ANGER

The discretion of a man makes him slow to anger, and his glory is to overlook a transgression. (Proverbs 19:11)

O f course, you never get angry. Right? No, wrong! Unless you are nigh onto perfect, you have moments of anger now and then. And some of you seem to stay angry. Yes, I have my moments of anger. You will also discover there is a good and righteous anger. But unrighteous anger is the acid which destroys its container.

There are four concepts I want you to pick up as we deal with God's answer to anger. And I pray to God the Holy Spirit will write these truths on the tablets of your heart—because there is probably nothing that damages us more physically, emotionally, or spiritually, than anger. An ungoverned, uncontrollable temper can sour and poison our lives.

SUDDEN ANGER MUST BE CONTROLLED

Are you the kind of a person who gets suddenly angry? You alibi, "Well, I've got red hair." Or, "I'm Irish." Maybe you even brag about your short fuse. You are like a loaded shotgun with a hair trigger, ready to go off the moment you are jostled. Some people are almost proud of that. But if you are one of them, I want to show you what the Bible says about people who lose their tempers. Actually they don't *lose* their tempers—they really *find* it! But these people are quickly jarred and speedily set off, and they rapidly fly into a rage.

By the way, Will Rogers mused, "People who fly into a rage seldom make a good landing." So, pay attention.

Let's walk through the book of Proverbs for a while. God hasn't lumped all these Scriptures together so we must search them out. Proverbs 14:17a says, "A quick tempered man acts foolishly." That means: if you are a person with an ungovernable temper you are foolish. Remember it wasn't I that called you a fool—it was God.

Or look at 15:18, "A wrathful man stirs up strife, but he who is slow to anger allays contention." A sure way to pick a fight is to have a quick temper. A certain way to an argument is to fly off the handle.

Look at 25:8, "Do not go hastily to court, for what will you do in the end, when your neighbor has put You to shame?" Don't start arguing and don't become angry before you hear the whole matter. Don't talk when you ought to be listening. The Bible says, "When the wicked comes, contempt comes also; and with dishonor comes reproach" (Proverbs 18:13). You can so easily jump at conclusions.

"Once there was a dog named August who was always jumping at conclusions. One day he jumped at the conclusion of a mule. That was the last day of August." That's the message of this Scripture. You may start something you don't understand and end up in genuine trouble.

Look in Proverbs 29:20. This is a theme presented many times in the Word of God. "Do you see a man hasty in his words? There is more hope for a fool than for him." If you are a person who is quick to anger and hasty with your words, you will have to improve in order to reach the level of a fool! God said that.

There is so much you can lose when you fly into a rage. Many times you have no idea what you are saying. I heard of a man standing on a street corner with two other gentlemen waiting on a bus. An automobile came by, and the car went into the water left standing from a recent rain. The water and the mud splashed onto the fresh-pressed suit of this man standing there on the street corner. He turned to the two men standing by him and exclaimed, "Did you two fools see what that gentleman did to me?"

We lose our temper and begin to talk before we even think. Proverbs 19:19a says, "A man of great wrath will suffer punishment." There is so much to lose.

You can lose your friends; they may not tolerate your antics. You can lose your job; you can tell off the boss if you want to (but I don't recommend it if you'd like to keep your job). You can lose your wife; she may walk out on you. You can lose your children, they may disown you. You can lose your health. Ad infinitum.

When you become angry, psychological and physiological changes take place in your body. Your body begins to pump adrenaline into your blood. Your heart begins to beat faster; your blood pressure rises; your eyes dilate; your mouth gets dry; and the palms of your hands get sweaty. Your knees, your elbows, and your hands start to tremble. And these changes are not good for you. They do you all kinds of severe damage.

John Hunter, the physiologist who had a heart condition, said: "The first scoundrel that gets me angry will kill me." He died from anger! Anytime you become needlessly angry, you're just driving another nail into your coffin.

"A man of great wrath will suffer punishment" (Proverbs 19:19a). And so, if you've got a short fuse, if you are a person who is given to quick flashes of temper, you had better heed the Word of God. How can you do that?

Confess Your Anger

First of all, you ought to confess that you are getting angry. That's hard for some of us to do. We feel those feelings stirring, but, after all, we're Christians. And we don't want anybody to know we're getting angry. And we won't even confess it to ourselves. We won't admit it. We merely try to repress it.

When you repress it, that's like taking a trash can full of paper, setting it on fire, putting it into the closet, shutting the door, and saying. "It's not there." One of two things will happen: It will either burn out or it will burn the house down. Sometimes it will burn out, but other times it will burn until it does irrevocable damage.

You need not repress it or express it, but confess it. Admit it's there. You are not going to receive help until you admit you need help. When there is something stirring in you, something moving in you that you do not like, prayerfully confess: "Lord, I've got some bad feelings coming up in me."

Consider Your Anger

And then after you confess it, consider it. Ask, "Lord, show me what it is. Why am I getting so mad?" You've heard people remark, "Count to ten when you get angry and then speak." Well, if you are real angry, count to one hundred and don't say anything!

Now how do you consider it while you're counting? Look in Proverbs 14:29, "He who is slow to wrath has great understanding, but he who is impulsive exalts folly." That means if you will just slow down, become slow to get angry, God will give you understanding. You will be able to think the situation through. You will be able to discern what it is that's making you angry, and whether or not you have a right and a cause to be angry.

Control Your Anger

You say, "I can't control it." Don't tell me you can't control it. You can control it. Proverbs 29:11 says, "A fool vents all his feelings, but a wise man holds them back." That means he can do it. A wise man doesn't say everything he thinks. He doesn't go spouting off. He keeps it in.

Have you ever been in one of those family "discussions?" We don't call them arguments. They are just discussions that can be heard two blocks away!

The husband is yelling at the wife and the wife is yelling at the husband. They are snarling and fighting, and then the phone rings. You pick it up and answer, "Hellooo." You're so sweet. Isn't it amazing how you can turn it off—just like that? You reply, "I can't control it." Then how did you answer the phone so sweetly? You can control it, and you know you can control it.

Let me tell you, when you find yourself suddenly getting angry—if you'll not take the word of Adrian Rogers, then take the Word of God that teaches you are to be slow to wrath. A man of discretion defers his anger. He puts it off. He gives it time. He says, "Lord, I'm getting angry. Lord show me what it is that's making me angry. And, Lord, give me self-control and discipline that only You can give."

Flying off the handle is a dreadfully dangerous thing. So, remember: if you are a person who cannot control sudden anger there is going to be little hope for your ability to get along in life.

Sudden anger must be controlled. Don't say it can't be controlled when God's Word tells you repeatedly not to get angry in a hurry. God has never commanded you to do something you can't do with His help. Behind every command of God is His omnipotent power to carry out that command. Anything God commands me to do, He enables me to do.

SINFUL ANGER IS TO BE CONDEMNED

Our text in Proverbs 19:11 speaks of a man of discretion. That means a man who defers his anger. He puts it off and thinks about it. "Why am I angry? What is eating at me?"

If he determines that his anger is sinful anger, immediately it is to be condemned. Don't be easy on yourself at this point. Call it what it is. It is not weakness; it is wickedness. You contend, "Well, it just runs in my family." That's right, it does if you are of your father the devil!

Don't blame heredity. Don't blame circumstances. There is one thing God will not accept for sin, and that is an alibi. Anger is a horrible, hellish, hurtful sin. Sudden anger must be controlled. Sinful anger must be condemned.

How can you tell whether or not your anger is sinful? Let me just give you a few check points.

1. *If you don't have sufficient cause, your anger is sinful.* Jesus said, "But I say to you that whoever is angry with his brother without a cause shall be in danger of the judgment" (Matthew 5:22a). Many times we are angry and there is no legitimate reason for that anger. That problem is the frustration in us and we express it by striking out at other people. Anger without a cause is sinful anger.

2. *Anger against a person rather than against an injustice or against an offense is sinful anger.* We are to love people; we are to love the sinner, even though we do not love his sin. But if your anger is focused upon a person and you've come to hate a person, that is sinful anger.

3. *If you have a desire for revenge, you want to get even, that is sinful anger.* The Bible says, "'Vengeance is Mine; I will repay,' says the Lord" (Romans 12:19b).

Anger is sinful when it is cherished. If you don't want to give it up, or you dearly love your anger, or you think you have a right to it, then it is sinful anger.

If you have anger accompanied by an unforgiving spirit, or there is somebody who has wronged you and you don't wish to forgive them, it is sinful anger. I don't care what they did. It doesn't matter if at the beginning it was justified or unjustified—if there is an unforgiving spirit in your heart, it is sinful anger. And so, dear friend it must be condemned and repented of the moment it enters your heart.

Sudden anger is to be controlled. Don't fly off the handle. *Sinful anger is to be condemned.* Don't treat it as a weakness; treat it as a wickedness, as horrible sin. Confess it, repent of it, repudiate it, ask God to cleanse you and forgive you.

STUBBORN ANGER IS TO BE CONQUERED

Stubborn anger is terrible. Look again at our text in Proverbs 19:11, "A fools vents all his feelings, but a wise man holds them back." One of the most glorious things you can do is to pass over a transgression. Pass over what has hurt you, what has wounded you. To forgive, to restore, to make it right again.

There is a New Testament passage which deals with stubborn anger. It is in the book of Ephesians 4:26-27. Here is an unusual command, "Be angry, and do not sin, do not let the sun go down on your wrath, nor give place to the devil." I imagine you didn't know that you were commanded to be angry. We'll talk about that in just a moment.

There are some people who have learned to live with their anger. Some of you have been angry for ten or fifteen years. You have a stubborn anger. And the sun will rise and set and rise and set again upon that same anger. You have an unforgiving spirit. Someone has done you wrong, and your anger burns.

Sometimes husbands and wives have a spat and they go to bed back to back. Have you ever done that? You don't get out of bed, you don't pray, you don't get down on your knees, and ask each other's forgiveness and God's forgiveness. But you let the sun go down upon your wrath.

What are you doing when you act like that? You are saying, "Devil, you are welcome to come in, wreck our home, ruin our health, kill our happiness, negate our testimony, and destroy our lives."

The Bible says, "do not let the sun go down upon your wrath, nor give place to the devil." When a person has stubborn anger in his heart he just says, "Devil, come on in. You're welcome. Here is your place, devil." And that stubborn anger becomes the foul nest where the devil is going to hatch more eggs. That stubborn anger becomes the foxhole out of which the devil is going to snipe at your life. That stubborn anger becomes the beachhead from which the devil is going to attack and take more and more ground.

The devil sees an open door and he will go right through it. When you let the sun go down upon your wrath you have given place to the devil.

Now let me show you how the devil, the enemy, works when you give him a place. Look at verse 31 of Ephesians 4: "Let all bitterness, wrath, anger, clamor, and evil speaking, be put away from you, with all malice."

Now let's slow down because here are *six steps to disaster*. Here is what the devil does. Here's the anatomy of a horrible experience.

The Anatomy Of Anger

1. *Bitterness.* What is bitterness? Bitterness is that feeling of resentment we have when we think we've been wronged. Perhaps somebody has failed to do something for us, somebody has said something about us or didn't say something to us, whatever it is. Somehow we get in our heart that "I-have-been-wronged" feeling. And that is what the Bible calls bitterness.

The book of Hebrews calls it "a root of bitterness" (12:15b). Have you tried to weed your lawn in the spring and deal with dandelions? You try to pull them up and what happens? The root stays in the ground. All you're doing is pruning the leaves and strengthening the roots! And they come back up in a few days stronger than ever, because you haven't really dealt with the matter. All you have dealt with is the expression of the matter, the leaves, but you haven't dealt with the root of the matter.

The Bible says, "[Beware] lest any root of bitterness springing up cause trouble, [because it will defile your soul]" (Hebrews 12:15). That is, your psyche. And that root of bitterness is there. That's what the devil starts with. He wants you to feel you've been wronged. Somebody's done you wrong, and you have that resentment. And when we don't deal with it, we give a place to the devil.

2. *Wrath.* The word *wrath* here comes from a Greek word which means "to burn." We begin to do a slow burn. Have you ever done it? Don't look so pious. A slow burn. That is, we get hot and bothered. There is a fire that starts inside. It comes right on the heels of that bitterness, and it smolders in the heart.

3. *Anger.* This is the next step in Ephesians 4:31. Anger does not refer to that which is on the inside like the word *wrath*, but anger now refers to that which is on the outside.

We get angry and we begin to show it now by the expression on our face, by the narrowing of the eyes, and by the physiological and psychological manifestations that occur in us. The wrath which has been smoldering now bursts into open flames in the attic of our mind.

4. *Clamoring.* Now the word *clamor* means what it sounds like. It means loud speech. It may be crying; it may be shouting. Have you ever noticed when we get angry we tend to get loud? You advise a person, "You don't have to shout." And he yells, "I'M NOT SHOUTING!" And he gets angry. And because he is angry he gets loud and red in the face. He gets clamorous.

But the devil is not finished with him yet. You see, he opened the door with that bitterness. The devil is really working now. And so after the clamor comes the evil speaking.

5. *Evil Speaking.* When you raise your voice and get loud, you are doing exactly the opposite of the Scripture that says, "A soft answer turns away wrath, but a harsh word stir up anger" (Proverbs 15:1). And when you hear yourself speaking that way it reinforces itself. You begin to say things you don't mean.

You say slanderous things to a person you love. You may say "I hate you." "I wish we'd never gotten married." "You're such a miserable child." "You'll never amount to anything." We speak all kinds of cruel, harsh, and cutting words—words that we do not even mean. We know while we are speaking them they are wrong. But we are on a roll. And the devil says, "Yeah, and tell him this, too." And you say, "OK."

You had that stubborn anger, and so the devil takes that bitterness and he turns it into wrath and he turns that wrath into anger and he turns that anger into clamor and he turns that clamor into evil speaking and slander. But he's not yet finished because there is one more step downward.

6. *Malice.* This means a desire to hurt and to harm. If you are a bully you may reach out and hit somebody. You can be a female bully and slap a child. You can be a male bully and hit your wife. Or you can use a gun, a knife, or an automobile. You can do it financially or you can do it psychologically. But there is a desire to hurt someone. How ugly that is.

And the whole time it is going on, guess who is sitting in the corner with a big smile on his face? The old devil. And you said, "Come on in." You're the one that opened the door. You're the one that gave a place to the devil because of that stubborn anger.

Sudden anger must be controlled. Sinful anger must be condemned. Stubborn anger must be conquered. You can conquer. How are you going to do it? Proverbs 16:32 says, "He who is slow to anger is better than the mighty, and he who rules his spirit than he that takes a city."

You're not to be ruled by your spirit. You are to rule your spirit. You're not to be conquered. You are to be a conqueror. The Bible says, "We are to reign in this life by Christ Jesus" (see Romans 5:17).

Four Steps To Conquer Stubborn Anger

1. *Recognize Your Anger.* You must recognize that a root of bitterness is there. And you must trace it all the way back to the stubbornness. Unless you become honest with God and honest with yourself in getting down to the root of the matter, you are never going to deal with it.

2. *Repent Of Your Anger.* The Bible says in Ephesians 4:31 that you are to put away these things. That means to have a change of mind, to say, "I'm sick of it. I'm tired of it. I repent of it. I choose against it."

Nobody is going to choose for you, and God is not going to force it on you. You must repent. You must deal ruthlessly with this thing called anger. If you don't, it's going to destroy you and those you love.

3. *Renounce The Devil.* Remember you gave the devil a place. And, so, after you recognized that root of bitterness and dealt with it, saying, "God I repent of it. I change my mind. I'm wrong. I have no right to be this angry, this upset," you must continue. After you repent of it, then you can say to the devil, "Devil, I gave you some territory and now I'm taking it back. And I resist you. I rebuke you. I renounce you. Be gone out of my life." And kick him out.

You say, "Can I kick him out?" Absolutely! You can kick him out in the name of Jesus. The Bible says, "Resist the devil and he will flee from you. Draw near to God and He will draw near to you..." (James 4:7b, 8a).

Once you've cleansed that ground, once you've dealt with that root of bitterness, once you've recognized it and once you've repented of it, you can renounce the devil and say to him in no uncertain terms, "Devil, you have no right in my life. I'm a Christian. I'm saved. My sins are under the blood. I've dealt with that root of bitterness. And this body of mine, this mind of mine, this whole soul of mine, and this spirit of mine is a temple of God's Holy Spirit. It doesn't belong to you. And you are trespassing on my Father's property. And in the name of Jesus, be gone."

The Bible says, "Resist the devil, and he will flee from you." Do you believe that? I do. But you are going to have to deal with him. Say, "Satan, you're out, you're gone. I stand against you in the full name of Jesus and the power of His blood."

4. *Rely Upon The Holy Spirit.* The passage in Ephesians goes on to say, "And be kind to one another, tenderhearted, forgiving one another, even as God in Christ forgave you" (4:32). Rely upon God's Holy Spirit to come into you and give you that love, that kindness, and that tenderheartedness.

The next time you need to love an enemy don't say, "Lord, help me to love my enemy." Just say, "Your love, Lord." He will *love through you.* He will *forgive through you.* And you can conquer stubborn anger.

Now the fourth and final thing I want to say, not only must sudden anger be controlled, sinful anger be condemned, and stubborn anger be conquered, *but sanctified anger needs to be channeled.*

SANCTIFIED ANGER NEEDS TO BE CHANNELED

It is not always a sin to be angry. As a matter of fact, we've already read where the Bible says in Ephesians 4:26a, "Be angry, and do not sin." If it's always a sin to be angry then Jesus was a sinner because Jesus became angry. You say, "Sure enough?" Yes, let me show you.

> And He entered the again, and a man was there who had a withered hand. So they watched Him closely, whether He would heal him on the Sabbath, so that they might accuse Him. And He said to the man who had the withered hand, 'Step forward.' Then He said to them, 'Is it lawful on the Sabbath to do good or to do evil, to save life or to kill?' But they kept silent. And when He had looked around at them with anger, being grieved by the hardness of their hearts, He said to the man, 'Stretch out your hand.' And he stretched it out, and his hand was restored as whole as the other. (Mark 3:1-5)

Who is "they?" That refers to the Pharisees. They hated Jesus. They didn't care about this man with the withered hand. The milk of human kindness had curdled in the Pharisees, "And they watched Him."

Now Jesus was without sin, and yet Jesus was not without anger. What angered the Lord Jesus Christ was not what someone else had done to Him. You will never find Jesus retaliating when somebody does something to Him. He doesn't retaliate. As a matter of fact, Jesus always returned good for evil.

And you don't find Jesus trying to get even. Jesus did not get angry even when they nailed Him to the cross. But what angered Jesus was insensitivity to the hurts and needs of other people.

These Pharisees were filled with selfishness, pride, and greed. They despised Jesus because they felt He was a usurper. They jealously felt Jesus was horning in on the hold they previously had on the people. They cared nothing for that poor man with the withered hand.

That angered Jesus. The Lord became justifiably angry when He saw people being abused, misused, and stepped on. Anger is not always the opposite of love. The fact is—at times it is the best expression of love! When you love with heavenly love through the Holy Spirit, and you see people being hurt, it ought to make you angry.

The liquor traffic ought to make you angry. The peddlers of pornography ought to make you angry. Those who mistreat other people, showing them no love or respect, ought to make you intensely angry. People who manipulate and abuse little children should stir you to anger.

Under those circumstances, if you cannot get angry, your character is lacking. There is an appropriate time for the right kind of anger motivated by the Lord Jesus. The Word makes it plain, "Be angry and sin not." Your anger needs to be holy, righteous anger. Not anger at a person but at their sins.

If you are against pornography, you are still to love the pornographer. The big difference between you and him is Jesus—that's it—Jesus. Oppose their filthy, evil traffic, but love them in Jesus' name. The way to be angry and sin not is to be angry at sin.

You reply, "But wait a minute. How can you hate the sin and still love the sinner? It's impossible." No, it's not. Let me ask you. Do you ever become angry with your own misdeeds? Do you ever say to yourself, "You're stupid!"? If you're human you probably do, or at least you have at one time or another. Yet don't you love you? You know, the guy I have so much trouble with is my wife's husband! I get angry at what I do, but I love me. As a matter of fact, it's because I love me that I get angry at what I do.

Sometimes we become angry over our children when we are afraid they are ruining and wasting their lives, their talents, their potential for Christ. Why? Because we love them so much.

We must have righteous anger. Take the Christian who is a limp dishrag. He wants no trouble. He doesn't want to "make waves." He doesn't want to get involved. Frankly, he could stand an infusion of holy anger. Remember, the Lord Jesus, the holy, perfect, righteous Son of God, God Himself, was angry when heavenly holiness called for it.

Godly anger is like that of the Lord Jesus, an anger that does something about the problem. In the book of Mark, the Lord Jesus healed a man and helped a man. Where there is holy anger, one is angry at the right time for the right reason and in the right place.

Were it not for irate Christians, we would have sweat shops where little children slave sixteen hours a day, seven days a week. Were it not for righteous indignation, slavery would be practiced in the Western World. Were it not for holy anger, women would be treated as chattel slaves.

In our cities across America we must have a baptism of righteous indignation. Some of you ladies ought to go into these convenience stores, pick up those girlie magazines, carry them to the manager, and insist, "What do you mean by this? How dare you?" Scare the dollars right out of their pockets. And we Christians ought to mount up an attack against the pernicious evil of gambling which destroys thousands of lives.

What caused a certain chain store to drop profitable girlie magazines from its racks? You guessed it. Christian organizations composed of indignant people who were tired of buying a half-gallon of milk or a loaf of bread and being bombarded with filth staring them and their children square in the face.

Many have protested, "That's what we pay our pastor to do. Pastor, go out there and fight the devil and his crowd. We are behind you 100 percent. We are with you to the last drop of your blood." When enough godly people become indignant about the sins that are destroying the lives of our citizens, it might well turn our nation around.

I am not referring to going off half-cocked. I am not speaking of unrighteous anger and uncontrolled anger. I have in mind the anger of our Lord Jesus Christ when He found people crushed and downtrodden. Jesus became angry, but He never sinned. We must become angry and not sin.

From the Word of God it is plain that we are not to have uncontrolled anger. We are to confess that kind of anger, consider it, and control it with the aid of the blessed Holy Spirit.

Sudden anger has to be condemned and conquered. I have mentioned that there are six steps to disaster unless anger is controlled. Bitterness or resentment. Wrath. Anger out of control. Clamor. Evil speaking and slander. Malice.

Finally, there are four steps to conquering your stubborn anger. Recognize it. Repent of it. Renounce the devil. Rely upon the Holy Spirit.

Sudden anger must be controlled. Sinful anger must be condemned. Stubborn anger must be conquered. And sanctified anger must be channeled.

What is God's answer to anger? "The discretion of a man makes him slow to anger, and his glory is to overlook a transgression." Who is our pattern about properly handling anger within our lives? None other than the Lord Jesus. He was despised and rejected of men, afflicted and smitten by His oppressors. Yet, He cried from the cross, "Father, forgive them, for they know not what they do." He never became angry when He was mistreated, but He did become angry when others were hurt and preyed upon.

Pray for all the beauty of Jesus to be reflected in you. Love like Jesus. Pray like Jesus. Walk in His steps. And be righteously angry like Jesus.

Albert Orsborn wrote:

Let the beauty of Jesus be seen in me,
All His wonderful passion and purity;
O Thou Spirit divine,
All my nature refine,
Till the beauty of Jesus is seen in me.

CHAPTER NINE

GOD'S MIRACLE MEDICINE

Anxiety in the heart of man causes depression, but a good word makes it glad. (Proverbs 12:25)

A merry heart makes a cheerful countenance, but by sorrow of the heart the spirit is broken. The heart of him who has understanding seeks knowledge, but the mouth of fools feed on foolishness. All the days of the afflicted are evil, but he who is of a merry heart has a continual feast. (Proverbs 15:13-15)

A merry heart does good, like medicine, but a broken spirit dries the bones. (Proverbs 17:22)

M y library contains a thick-spined volume written by a medical doctor, Dr. John A. Schindler (*How to Live 365 Days a Year*, New York: Prentice-Hall and Company, 1954). In it he discusses a sickness he refers to by the initials E.I.I. I wonder if you have it today. It stands for "emotionally induced illness." People are sick physically, but it is their emotions that have made them ill.

The renowned Dr. Schindler stated that 50 percent of the people who are treated by physicians are there because of E.I.I. Fifty percent! Every other bed in the hospital is there because of E.I.I.

In order to back up what he found, Dr. Schindler investigated some well-known clinics, including the famous Oschner Clinic in New Orleans. And in that clinic they tested five hundred consecutive patients who had been admitted with gastrointestinal problems. After the examinations, it was concluded that 74 percent of those patients had E.I.I.

Another study was conducted in the Outpatient Department of the Yale University Medical School. The conclusion again was that 76 percent of those coming to that department had E.I.I.

Dr. Schindler wrote that part of the problem is that the doctor is afraid to tell the patient he has an emotionally induced illness for fear he will become angry and demand another doctor. It is hard for a person to admit.

Then he went on to give an educated guess of the percentages of those with different illnesses who are in reality suffering from E.I.I. For example, he estimated that 75 percent of stiffness in the back of the neck is caused by E.I.I. Ninety percent of lumps in the throat and difficulty swallowing are caused by E.I.I. Fifty percent of light pain in the stomach is E.I.I.

He concluded that 94 44/100 percent of all gas and bloating is actually E.I.I. Dizziness, 80 percent. Headaches, 80 percent. And here's one—tiredness, 90 percent. Emotionally induced illnesses!

I want to give you a little G.M.M. —God's Miracle Medicine. What does God think about this?

Ponce de Leon, the Spaniard, came to Florida many years ago seeking the fountain of youth. He never found it. He should have looked in the book of Proverbs. Proverbs 17:22a says, "A merry heart does good, like medicine."

THE MISERY OF A HEAVY HEART

It Burdens The Soul

Anxiety in the heart of man causes depression. (Proverbs 12:25a)

The body, as well as the heart is bowed down with a load of care. It is a load you were never meant to carry.

An old story has frequently been told about a man walking down the road on a hot day burdened by a heavy sack of grain resting on his shoulders. Another man in an old buckboard pulled by a horse stopped and said, "Hey, it's too hot for you to be walking like that! Climb up here in the wagon, and I'll give you a lift."

The man with the load of grain on his shoulder climbed into the wagon and sat down. After a while the fellow with the reins looked over and insisted, "My goodness, sir! Put that grain down and relax!" "Oh, no," he answered, "It's enough to ask you to give me a ride without your carrying my load also."

Many people who would claim that was ridiculous have gotten into the wagon with Jesus for salvation but have never set their load down. They say, "Lord, I can trust You to save me, but I just can't trust You to carry this load." The Bible says, "Cast your burden on the LORD, and He shall sustain you" (Psalm 55:22). The old song puts it this way, "Take your burden to the Lord and leave it there."

It Breaks The Spirit

A merry heart makes a cheerful countenance, but by sorrow of the heart the spirit is broken. (Proverbs 15:13)

The spirit is that innermost part of a person. The spirit is the wellspring of life! It is the deepest part.

It's one matter to burden the soul. It's yet another to break the spirit. You can have a burdened soul and get over it, but, oh, when it breaks your spirit, you're in trouble.

Have you ever seen a person with a broken spirit? When the light goes out of the eyes, the spark dies, the enthusiasm, the zest, and the fight all go, and there is nothing left but the shell of a person. I've seen that happen.

General Douglas MacArthur, one of my heroes, spoke these words, "Youth is not a time of life. It is a state of mind. It is not a matter of red cheeks, red lips, and supple knees. It is a temper of the will, a quality of the imagination, a vigor of the emotion. It is a freshness of the deep springs of life.

"Youth means a temperamental predominance of courage over timidity, of the appetite for adventure over a life of ease. This often exists in a man of fifty more than in a boy of twenty. Nobody grows old by merely living a number of years. People grow old by deserting their ideals. Years may wrinkle the skin, but to give up enthusiasm wrinkles the soul. Worry, doubt, self-distrust, fear, and despair, these are the long, long, long years that bow the head and turn the growing spirit back to dust.

"You are as young as your faith, as old as your doubt. As young as your self-confidence, as old as your fears. As young as your hope, as old as your despair."

It Buries The Body

> A merry heart does good, like medicine, but a broken spirit dries the bones. (Proverbs 17:22)

The soul affects the spirit, and the spirit affects the body, and the body begins to wither and to decay. Eventually this body will die, not because of the hardening of the arteries, but because of the hardening of the attitudes! It dries the bones! The entire body is affected with emotionally induced illness, psychosomatic sickness.

Frederick II ruled over Sicily in the thirteenth century before the days of modern psychology. He wondered what kind of language children would speak if they were left to themselves with nobody to teach them any language. Being a despot, he decided to perform a cruel experiment.

He took certain newborn babies from their parents and put them in foster homes with the instruction that nobody was to speak a single word to those infants. They were not to hear one sound!

His perverted curiosity wanted to see what kind of language they would speak if no one spoke to them. He never found out, because within a year every one of those babies died.

After World War II in Germany, another harsh experiment was performed on one hundred orphans. Fifty of those children were placed in one orphanage, fifty in another. The first orphanage gave those children love and happiness and conviviality. But the other orphanage gave nothing but stern discipline. There was no laughter, no fun, no joy, no games.

All had the same heat, the same cooling, the same housing, the same clothes, the same exercise, and the same food. But after a year, the children where the joy and the happiness were, on the average were two inches taller than the other children and several pounds heavier. The other group was disease-ridden and sickly.

The misery of a heavy heart buries the body, causing many, many people to die prematurely.

THE MASTERY OF A HAPPY HEART

God has given us good medicine to master that misery. It is a merry heart.

The Scripture is not only talking about fun and games, although that's a part of the spin-off. That's one of the by-products. The Scripture is not talking about humor or laughter, although that is another spin-off.

Some people claim that Charles Haddon Spurgeon was the greatest preacher who ever lived. But one lady criticized Spurgeon for bringing humor into his messages. Spurgeon replied, "Oh, don't criticize me. If you only knew how much I held back you would praise me."

Spurgeon had that bubbling, effervescent joy that sometimes showed itself in humor and laughter. But when we're talking about a merry heart what the language actually means is joy! Not mere laughter, not mere joking, not just fun and games, but deep, abiding joy. The mastery of a happy heart is when that joy is there.

The Seat Of That Joy

For out of the abundance of the heart the mouth speaks. (Matthew 12:34b)

For as he thinks in his heart, so is he. (Proverbs 23:7a)

In Hebrew psychology, the heart is the core of the individual. And the seat of joy is in the heart. It does not depend upon things. It does not depend upon thrills. It comes from the heart. The devil generally starts from the outside and works in, but God starts from the inside and He works out.

The source of that joy. "And whoever trusts in the LORD, happy is he" (Proverbs 16:20b). The Lord Jesus Himself is the source of that joy. John 15:11 says, "These things have I spoken to you, that My joy may remain in you, and that your joy may be full."

Jesus spoke of His joy. We sing about Jesus as being "a man of sorrows and acquainted with grief." But do not ever paint a picture of Jesus as being a sanctimonious, pale, religious recluse. As a matter of fact, the Bible describing the Lord Jesus says, "Thou... hath anointed You with the oil of gladness above Thy fellows" (Hebrews 1:9). That means nobody who has ever lived had joy like the Lord Jesus.

And Jesus affirmed, "I'm going to give My joy to you" (see John 15:11). The joy I have today is not some cheap imitation of His joy. It's the real thing.

An article sometime back in the *Reader's Digest* said that man needs three things in order to make him happy and fulfilled. He needs someone to love, something meaningful to do, and something to hope for. That's pretty good, because Jesus is all three.

Someone to love: "We love Him because He first loved us" (1 John 4:19). Something to do: "Serve the LORD with gladness" (Psalm 100:2a). Something to hope for: "Looking for the blessed hope and glorious appearing of our great God and Savior Jesus Christ" (Titus 2:13).

To have Christ in your heart is to have that joy. And that joy is strong medicine.

Thankfully, Nehemiah had a dependable source. He wrote, "For the joy of the LORD is your strength" (Nehemiah 8:10b). And joy is indeed strong medicine. The *Executive Digest* said that even induced laughter gives you strength, affecting every organ of the body. But I am not speaking about forced laughter. I am talking about something far more potent than that, the joy of the Lord.

The poet Elizabeth Barrett was an invalid for many years, unable even to lift her head from her pillow. One day she was visited by a man named Robert Browning. In just one visit he gave her so much joy and happiness that she lifted her head from the pillow. On his second visit she sat up in bed. On the third visit they eloped. That's strong medicine. But the joy of the Lord is even stronger.

Medically, it is true. Dr. Schindler said that happy emotions affect the pituitary gland, which, in turn, affects the entire body. It secretes chemicals which are indeed medicine. Yet, in his book Dr. Schindler never referred to the Lord as the source of this desperately needed joy. He knew the problem. I know the solution.

The Stability Of That Joy

All the days of the afflicted are evil. (Proverbs 15:15a)

People laden with care are unable even to see the good things that happen to them. "But he who is of a merry heart has a continual feast" (Proverbs 15:15b). What a contrast.

Jesus said in John 15:11a, "These things have I spoken to you, that My joy may remain in you." That is, that it might be "stable." You need to understand that your joy is no better than the source of that joy.

If you get your joy from friends, if you get your joy from possessions, if you get your joy from your health or your business, you are getting your joy from things that can change.

This is not the case with the joy of Jesus. Facing the cross He was talking about His joy. His joy was self-contained. It was stable. "He that is of a merry heart hath a continual feast." His joy stays.

The devil has no happy old people. The poet Lord Byron lived high, wide, and handsome as a young man. He had looks, wit, and charm. Yet, even as a young man, Lord Byron wrote, "My days are in the yellow leaf; The flowers and fruits of love are gone; The worm, the canker, and the grief are mine alone!" He sought his joy in the wrong places. It did not last.

THE MINISTRY OF A HEALTHY HEART

God does not give us His joy and His strength so we can serve the devil. Of course not. He gives us this strength so we might minister.

This Joy Is To Be Sought

It is not automatic. You can have medicine in the cabinet, but you must take it. Day by day you must receive the joy of the Lord. We have already seen that "A merry heart maketh a cheerful countenance: but by sorrow of the heart, the spirit is broken." But look at the verse that follows it. "The heart of him who has understanding seeks knowledge" (Proverbs 15:14a).

You are to seek the Lord. Did you seek Him this morning with all your heart? Did you bathe yourself in His presence? Jesus said, "These things have I spoken unto you that [you might have joy]." What things? He taught that we are to abide in Him and He in us (see John 15:4).

A man wrote his congressman, asking, "Where is all this happiness that the Constitution of the United States guarantees us?" The congressman wrote back and suggested, "You better reread the Constitution. It doesn't guarantee you any happiness. It guarantees you the pursuit of happiness."

This is particularly true in the spiritual realm. "The heart of him who has understanding seeks knowledge" (Proverbs 15:14).

This Joy Is To Be Seen

A merry heart makes a cheerful countenance. (Proverbs 15:13a)

If you have joy in your heart it ought to show on your face. Do you know the reason you are so tired? It takes seventy-two muscles to frown and fourteen to smile. Look at all that wasted energy.

I like to read bumper stickers. You can almost tell who's who by reading their bumper stickers. At least, most of the time. I was riding down the road awhile back and I saw a bumper sticker that read, "Smile. God loves you." *Boy!* I thought, *a Christian. How wonderful.*

So I sped up and came alongside and looked in the window. The woman driving that car looked like she was having a gall bladder attack. I have never seen such misery written on the face of a woman. I thought to myself, *She needs to take that bumper sticker off the bumper and put it on the dashboard.* It ought to show on your face.

"It is this that made the future of Christianity," wrote Matthew Arnold, the famous British essayist. "Its gladness, not its sorrow... its drawing from the spiritual world a source of joy so abundant that it ran over upon the material world and transfigured it."

I received a letter from a lady I had never met, asking me to forgive her for a feeling she had toward me. And guess what she didn't like about me? You say, "I can't imagine." She wrote, "I thought you were a hypocrite. For years I've been watching you on television. You're always so happy. I just felt like nobody could be that happy all of the time. You had to be a fake."

And then she added, "Finally, after several years, I came to hear you in person. And I watched, and I listened. I visited with your people. Now I know it's real. I know it's real."

That's the joy of the Lord! I am not trying to suggest that you look at me because, friend, if there is anything good about me, I will guarantee you it is because of the Lord Jesus. And if there is any joy in me it is the joy of the Lord Jesus.

This Joy Is To Be Shared

This is how we will win the lost to Christ. One of the greatest testimonies we have is the joy of the Lord. A cold, dry faith has no appeal.

Some years ago I read about some gold prospectors out West who discovered a very rich mine. They exclaimed, "Hey, we've got it made as long as we don't tell anybody else before we stake our claims." And they made a vow of secrecy.

But they had to go into town for provisions and tools. When they left the town, a great host of people followed them because it was written all over their faces. It was impossible to hide what they had found.

This miracle medicine is of far more value than gold. If you knew the cure for some dread disease, wouldn't you share it? Wouldn't you tell it? I believe the joy of the Lord is there not only to strengthen us but also that we may transfer that joy to others. I believe it ought to be a common occurrence for people to come to us asking, "What is the reason for the hope that is within you?"

Without joy, life is meaningless. I care not what else you may have. And that joy is only found in Jesus. We ought to share the secret.

Patrick Henry, that redheaded Virginian who proclaimed "Give me liberty or give me death" wrote these words in his will. To those who were receiving his inheritance he advised, "There is one thing more I wish I could give you. It is the religion of our Lord Jesus Christ. With it, if you have nothing else, you could be happy. Without it, though you have all things else, you would not be happy."

True joy is found in the Lord Jesus. It is God's miracle medicine for E.I.I. Cyprian, one of the church's early leaders, wrote to a friend about this joy:

This is a cheerful world as I see it from my garden, under the shadow of my vines. But if I could ascend some high mountain and look out over the wide lands, you know very well what I would see—brigands on the highways; pirates on the seas; armies fighting; cities burning; in the amphitheaters men murdered to please applauding crowds; selfishness and cruelty; misery and despair under all roofs. It is a bad world.

But I have discovered in the midst of it a quiet and holy people who have learned a great secret. They have found a joy which is a thousand times better than any of the pleasures of our sinful life. They are despised and persecuted, but they care not. They have overcome the world. These people, Donatus, are the Christians—and I am one of them.

CHAPTER TEN

GOD'S GRACE IN THE WORK PLACE

In all labor there is profit. (Proverbs 14:23a)

H enri Amiel felt strongly about work as he observed: "It is work which gives flavor to life."

How would you like to transform your work from boredom to blessing, from monotony to meaning, from drudgery to dignity, from the same old grind to glory? You will be able to if you will grasp the dynamic truth I am about to share with you.

Some people do not enjoy their work; they just endure it. They think their jobs are meaningless. They suspect that some folks must have happy jobs with excitement and meaning—but not them. They simply draw their breath and draw their salary.

They wake up in the morning (or another time, if they are not on the day shift), maybe take a bath and freshen up. They stagger toward the kitchen and gulp down a cup of coffee, scalding their throat in the process, and choke down a piece of burnt toast. They run out the door and fight the traffic, finally arriving at work where they follow the same old routine day after day.

When the day is over they may head home or go out somewhere before finally reaching their living quarters. "Mr. Average Worker" goes home, takes a couple of aspirins (or worse), and sits down to watch the TV. Maybe he will discuss the day with his wife and then putter around the garage or yard. Then it's the same mechanistic doldrums all over again. The stuck record, the treadmill, the jammed tape.

It sounds like the old song of the late forties: "Up in the morning, out on the job... Fuss with my woman, toil for my kids, work 'til I'm wrinkled and grey." The song goes on to say, "But that lucky old sun has nothing to do but roll 'round heaven all day."

Nothing exciting. Nothing different. Nothing thrilling. It seems so humdrum and pedestrian.

Many of these workers love God and serve Him, but they have the idea that the only time they can serve God is when they are away from the work place. They want to get off from work so they can serve the living God. And so they give the prime time to their employer and the leftovers to God, maybe Wednesday nights and weekends to Him.

They are serving God sort of part time with the boss garnering the best hours. What they are trying to do is serve two masters, which, of course, Jesus taught no one can do (see Matthew 6:24).

And many of you reading this right now are guilty of doing what I call split-level living. If you are, I want you to receive this into your heart today. You may be a very ordinary person. You may think there is nothing exciting about you, but I want you to know that God loves ordinary people. He made mostly that kind. He must like them. They are His most repeated handiwork!

And as a matter of fact, 1 Corinthians 1:26 notes: "For you see your calling, brethren, that not many wise according to the flesh, not many mighty, not many noble, are called." God uses ordinary people.

But here is the secret. God takes ordinary people and gives them extraordinary power. He infuses them with His Holy Spirit. And then God puts those ordinary people into ordinary places. When God takes an ordinary person, and gives him extraordinary power, and then puts that ordinary person in an ordinary place with that extraordinary power, He does extraordinary things through that ordinary person. If you will learn this, it will transform your life!

We neatly divide life up into the secular and the sacred. Many people confess, "You know, pastor, if I could do what I would really like to do, I'd just like to get out of this job and serve God. I'd really love to be able to serve God full-time. If I could just quit what I'm doing it would be so wonderful to be like you."

Have you ever thought that? I pray God will help me to teach you: If you are a Christian living in the Spirit you are serving God full-time. If it is an honorable occupation, you are serving God full-time. Your work is to be the temple of your devotion and the platform for your witness.

We divide life up into the secular and the sacred, but the New Testament does not. In the Old Testament they did, but not in the New Testament. In the Old Testament there were priests and the rest of the people. In the New Testament we are all priests. In the Old Testament there was a Temple people attended. But Jesus said that you should worship "neither on this mountain, nor in Jerusalem... But the hour is coming, and now is, when the true worshipers will worship the Father in spirit and truth" (John 4:21a, 23a).

In the Old Testament they divided food into the clean and the unclean, but in the New Testament, "thus He spoke making all meats clean." In the Old Testament certain dates and days were set aside, but in the New every day is a holy day, and every place is a sacred place. And every job has dignity if it is honest, honorable work. Every Christian is a priest and a minister, and every Christian is doing full-time Christian service.

You may not believe that at this moment, but keep reading, and I believe you will. God's Word says, "In all labor there is profit" (Proverbs 14:23a). Now you may not be in an exciting position.

Your job may be in a factory screwing lids on tubes of toothpaste all day long. You may be working in an office as a clerk or pumping gasoline or digging ditches. But if you will learn what I have to share from the Word of God, it is going to turn whatever you are doing from drudgery into delight. It is going to transform that monotony into magnificence. You are going to find out that you are where God has placed you, and you are there for a specific purpose.

There are *three things* I want you to see. First, I want you to see the *sacredness of everyday work*. Second, I want you to see the sphere of everyday work. And third, I want you to see the *service of everyday work*.

THE SACREDNESS OF EVERYDAY WORK

Don't get the idea that to serve God you have to be a minister or a missionary or on the staff of some Christian organization. Every job, if it is done in the power of the Holy Spirit, is sacred. Every one.

Let me give you a verse: "Bondservants, be obedient to those who are your masters according to the flesh, with fear and trembling, in sincerity of heart, as to Christ" (Ephesians 6:5).

You are to work for your boss, "that two-legged devil," as though he were Jesus Christ Himself. That's right. It is God who owns the company that your boss thinks he owns. "This is my Father's world," and you are actually serving the Lord Jesus.

Daniel is a prime example. You will remember that Daniel was taken as a captive from Israel, and he was carried to Babylon by King Nebuchadnezzar. In Babylon, Daniel had the secular job of a government bureaucrat. They trained him, and they pressed him into the service of the government. But as a government bureaucrat he really served the Lord Jesus.

Daniel was neither a pastor nor a priest. Daniel was what we would call a businessman in ordinary work.

Remember Daniel refused to do certain things when he was in Babylon, and they threw him into the lions' den as punishment. But the lions got "lockjaw." And Daniel just relaxed and pulled up an old fluffy lion for a pillow, got out his Old Testament, and began to "read between the lions."

He was having a wonderful time there doing his devotions when the king looked in at him. Read the king's words in Daniel 6:20, "And when he came to the den, he cried out with a lamenting voice unto Daniel. The king spoke, saying to Daniel, Daniel, servant of the living God, has your God, whom you serve continually, been able to deliver you from the lions?" And of course, that God had been able to deliver him.

What point am I trying to make? Daniel had a secular job, and yet even his enemies and the unsaved people of this world had to admit that his secular job was really sacred, that he was actually serving God.

You may be a homemaker, and you might think, *What's this got to do with serving the Lord?* Friend, there is no higher occupation than serving the Lord by being a homemaker. One woman has these words hung over her kitchen sink, "Divine services held here three times a day." If you do those dishes in the name of Jesus, and in the power of the Holy Spirit, you will receive the same reward for doing that job that I receive for preaching the Gospel.

You may not believe it, and you may think your job is not important at all. You may think, *Nobody cares about me, nobody knows about me.* God does, even if you don't get to lead in "silent" prayer in the children's department. God knows about you, and God has His eye upon you. Even if you are in secular work you are serving the Lord Christ, according to the Bible. Therefore every Christian is in full-time Christian work. Never forget it.

THE SPHERE OF EVERYDAY WORK

The second fact I want you to learn is not only the sacredness of everyday work, but also *the sphere of everyday work.* Where are you called to do this everyday work?

You reply, "Well, if I'm going to do it, I sure would like to be in a Christian company. I sure would like to be surrounded by Christians. You just don't know the people I work with. I don't believe God wants me in this place. It must be nice for you to be around all those people in the church. They are always smiling and always praying and always praising God.

"About the only time I hear God's name mentioned where I work is when it is taken in vain. And, Preacher, you can't believe the obscene stories. And you can't know the awful cartoons and things that are passed around. You can't believe the flirtation and the way people dress and the way they talk. And the greed and the dog-eat-dog and the ambition and the throat cutting and all of the materialism and the gossip that goes on. Oh, Pastor, if God would only free me from this place so I could serve Him."

It was God who put you in that place so you could serve Him! God put Daniel in Babylon.

Some of you are thinking, *Now, you know, Preacher, you talk about being called to your work. God called you to the ministry. Oh, if God would just call me. But God didn't call me. I'm just where I am as a victim of circumstances. To be very honest with you, Pastor, I took this job because it was the only one I could get. I just had to have it. And I don't know what I would do right now if I quit this job. I don't know where I'd go. And so, I have to stay here. But I don't have a sense of call. I don't have a sense of meaning. It is simply something I have to do because I've got to eat. Oh, would to God that I had a sense that God placed me where I am!*

Well, friend, God may have placed you where you are, and you were not aware of it. I want to ask you a question. Was Daniel a servant of God? Indeed, he was. Did Daniel serve God? Indeed he did. Was he where God wanted him? Indeed, he was. How did he get there? By circumstances beyond his control.

He was picked up by King Nebuchadnezzar, and he was brought as an exile into the land of Babylon, that place of wickedness. But how did he really get there? Jeremiah 29:4 tells us, "Thus saith the Lord of hosts, the God of Israel, unto all that are carried away captives, whom I have caused to be carried away from Jerusalem unto Babylon."

Did you see that? God makes it plain, "To all you who were carried away, I did it." Old Nebuchadnezzar thought he was doing it. The people who went thought they were victims of circumstances. *But where man rules, God overrules.*

You may think you are swept up in circumstances. You are there in a specific job, you have a particular background, and you may think it all just happened, and that there was no particular sense of call. But God has more than one way to place His people.

Now, God indeed may call you out of what we refer to as secular work into what we think of as the ministry. And God may say, "I don't want you in that factory anymore, I want you to be a preacher." God may say, "I want you to leave that office and become a missionary." But listen, dear friend, you are no more in full-time Christian work after you become a preacher than you were before.

I want to communicate with all the emphasis and unction and function and emotion of my soul that it is true! If you are walking in the Spirit, whether you are a farmer or whether you are a beautician, it doesn't make any difference. If it is a clean, honest occupation that is the place where God wants you. That is the sphere of your ministry, and it is full-time Christian service.

So many times you may cry, "God, I want to get out of Babylon. Lord, I want to do something for You. I want to get away from this worldly influence."

God's plan for you is not to flee from the world. God's plan for you is to confront the world and to overcome the world and to witness to the world. Jesus interceded in John 17:15, "I do not pray that You should take them out of the world, but that You should keep them from the evil one."

God's plan is not that you be taken out of that worldly environment, but that you live a good Christian life in it. First Corinthians 5:9-10 says, "I wrote to you in my epistle not to keep company with sexually immoral people. Yet I certainly did not mean with the sexually immoral people of this world, or with the covetous, or extortioners, or idolaters, since then would need to go out of the world."

Paul explained that if you tried to live your life without coming in contact with anybody who is dishonest, perverted, or sexually immoral you would have to move to another planet. You couldn't live here. You'd have to relocate to Mars.

This world is where we live, and God has placed us here. Romans 12:21 says, "Do not be overcome by evil, but overcome evil with good." We're not to flee from the world; we're to confront the world. First John 5:4 promises: "For whatever is born of God overcomes the world. And this is the victory that has overcome the world - our faith."

God has placed you in Babylon. God put Daniel in Babylon. And in the work you do there, as Daniel served the Lord God, you are to serve Him likewise. "In all labor there is profit."

That doesn't mean you can do everything in Babylon. That doesn't mean when you are in Babylon, do as the Babylonians do. Jesus said, "I do not pray that You should take them out of the world, but that You should keep them from the evil one."

There were certain things in Babylon that Daniel refused to do. Therefore he was thrown into the lions' den. There were certain things Daniel's friends, Shadrach, Meshach, and Abednego, refused to do. Therefore they were thrown into the fiery furnace. They received cruel persecution.

There are some things you cannot do. That is what is going to make you distinctively different. And that is what is going to make you so effective when you are in Babylon.

You have been saved out of the world and then sent back into the world to witness to the world, and that is the only business in the world you have in the world, until you are taken out of the world. We are called as Christians to confront this world with the Gospel of Jesus Christ.

We have a custom around our churches that is kind of artificial. We summon folks to the church on a certain night, give them a card, and tell them to go out and witness. There is a better method. And that is to witness every day for the Lord Jesus Christ on your job. We call this "lifestyle evangelism."

It is not that you pick some names and go across town to visit someone you don't know, but that you work side by side, day by day, with those you do know. And you let your light shine there in that dark place where God has placed you.

Jesus reminds us, "You are the light of the world. A city that is set on an hill cannot be hidden. Nor do they light a lamp and put it under a basket, but on a lampstand, and it gives light to all that are in the house" (Matthew 5:14-15).

For a light to be valuable it must be visible. Therefore God does not want you under a basket called a church house. God wants that light where it can be seen. Your job is the lampstand God has ordained for you to use in order to let your light shine.

Look at Philippians 2:15, "That you may become blameless and harmless, children of God without fault in the midst of a crooked and perverse generation, among whom you shine as lights in the world."

Where is the light to shine? In the middle of a crooked and perverse generation. It may not be God's will to remove you from that ungodly place where you work. You are to shine as lights in the world in the middle of a crooked and perverse nation.

If you were going to build a lighthouse, where would you build it? In downtown Manhattan? Of course not. You would build a lighthouse out on some rocky, craggy, barren coast so that lighthouse can help some ship that is about to go under. And that rocky, craggy, barren place is where God has placed you.

Daniel's friends were thrown into that fiery furnace for refusing to compromise their beliefs in Babylon, that crooked and perverse nation. Then Nebuchadnezzar realized God was God.

Look at his words in Daniel 3:28-29,

> Nebuchadnezzar spoke, saying, Blessed be the God of Shadrach, Meshach, and Abednego, who sent His Angel and delivered His servants who trusted in Him, and they have frustrated the king's word, and yielded their bodies, that they should not serve nor worship any god except their own God. Therefore I make a decree that any people, nation, or language which speaks anything amiss against the God of Shadrach, Meshach, and Abednego shall be cut in pieces, and their houses shall be made an ash heap: because there is no other God that can deliver like this.

That's a pagan king speaking. How would that king have ever known the power of God had it not been for Daniel and his three friends who used their secular jobs as a lampstand to let their lights shine in the midst of a crooked and perverse generation?

Jesus calls us to go into all the world. That includes the world of finances, business, and sports. In every world we are to go in and let our light shine for the Lord Jesus Christ.

Let me give you two other verses. Look at 1 Peter 2:11-12:

> Beloved, I beg you as sojourners and pilgrims, abstain from fleshly lusts which war against the soul, having your conduct honorable among the Gentiles, that when they speak against you as evildoers, they may, by your good works which they observe, glorify God in the day of visitation.

The lost world is to observe your life. Let your light shine. I wish you could only see that what you do is service to the Lord Jesus. If you could only see that God has placed you there in Babylon. That is the sphere of your witness. When people observe Christians living the Christian life on Monday, they will begin to believe what the preachers are preaching on Sunday.

Let me suggest four rules for witnessing to those with whom you work. I hope you are saying, "OK, Preacher, look out. Monday morning, here I come."

Number one rule, don't brag. The Bible says, "*Let* your light shine." Don't *make* it shine. It is to glow, not glare. They are to see the light, not the candle. If you go in there with a super load of self-righteousness, bragging about yourself, bragging about your church, bragging about your righteousness, and bragging about your doctrines, you are going to make them want to vomit. They are going to be sick of it. There is nothing worse than self-righteousness. Don't brag.

Second rule, don't nag. If you are always thumping a Bible, handing out a tract, preaching to somebody when he gambles, drinks, smokes, or curses, you aren't going to win anybody to Jesus Christ. You may think you are doing a good job, but what you are really doing is chasing them away.

You are not going to win an unsaved man that way because that is not his problem. You might be just like that man if you didn't know the Lord Jesus Christ. His major problem is that he just needs Jesus. Those are the only things he gets his kicks out of. He doesn't have the joy that you have. And you are not going to nag him to the Lord Jesus Christ.

As a matter of fact, look at Colossians 4:5-6, "Walk in wisdom toward those who are outside, redeeming the time. Let your speech always be with grace, seasoned with salt, that you may know how you ought to answer each one." If you could only say, "Salt my speech, Lord, season it with grace. I don't want to nag these people."

Third, don't lag. Do your part of the job. If you are a lazy Christian, if you are not getting there on time, if you are not doing the work you ought to do, you are a disgrace to grace! It's a sin for a Christian to do less than his best.

Look at Ephesians 6:5-6, "Servants, be obedient to them that are your masters according to the flesh, with fear and trembling, in singleness of your heart, as unto Christ; not with eyeservice, as men-pleasers, but as bondservants of Christ, doing the will of God from the heart."

You aren't to check to see if the boss is looking before you work hard. But instead you ought to look at that job, regardless of how dull and boring it may seem, as a service for Jesus. And don't be a laggard.

The Bible says in Colossians 3:23, "And whatever you do, do it heartily, as to the Lord and not to men." That will put a dignity in whatever it is you are doing. If you are running a machine, or greasing automobiles, or cutting yards, simply pray: "Jesus, I'm doing this for You, and I'll do it with all my might."

I can't think of anything that ought to put more of a spring in your step. You will be able to say, "I'm serving God as much this morning as Adrian Rogers does when he stands behind his pulpit. I am serving God as much as any missionary in the heart of deepest Africa."

A curious passerby watched three men working on an edifice.

He asked the first man, "What are you doing, sir?"

"Working for so much money a day."

He asked the same question of the second.

"Why, I'm cutting stone."

But when he asked the third, the workman replied with excitement, "I am building a cathedral in which thousands of people will praise and worship God Almighty!"

Reader, are you only working for so much money a day? If dedicated to God, pumping gas, frying hamburgers, turning bolts, operating sewing machines, driving a bus, or running a gigantic corporation is a service of adoration and praise to God.

Rule number four, don't let down. Don't lapse back into the ways of this world. Don't begin to complain. Don't get unhappy. Stay happy and full of joy. The only way to stay full of joy is to stay full of Jesus. That means you need to have a quiet time before you ever go to work in order to be filled up on the grace of God. You need to bathe yourself in the presence of Jesus. And when everybody else is griping and complaining and bellyaching, you can be there with the light of the Lord God upon your face.

Let me mention a thought about those people you work with. Most of them are not all that interested in going to heaven or to hell. They want to know how to hack it on Monday. And when they see you come into the office without a hangover and with the joy of the Lord Jesus on your face, after a while they are going to ask, "Hey, what's your secret?"

First Peter 3:15 says, "But sanctify the Lord God in your hearts, and always be ready to give a defense to everyone who asks you a reason for the hope that is in you, with meekness and fear."

You will not have to grab him by the buttonholes and probe, "Buddy, are you ready to meet God?" He is going to come to you. And he is going to inquire, "What on earth makes you tick? What is the secret of your life? Where are you getting that joy?" And because the joy of Jesus is real, and you've sanctified the Lord God in your heart, you are going to be able to share the Lord Jesus with him.

That's the sphere of everyday work. Right there in Babylon. God put Daniel in Babylon. He didn't have any special call from God. It was circumstances that put him there, but God was overruling, and that became Daniel's temple of devotion and his platform for witness. And Daniel touched a whole nation for God just by being God's man where God placed him.

I've shown you the sacredness of everyday work and the sphere of everyday work: now let me show you the *service of everyday work.*

THE SERVICE OF EVERYDAY WORK

By now I might have convinced some of you that the job you do is a platform to witness for the Lord Jesus. But I am sure there are others who are thinking, *I'm not even around anybody where I work. I spend all day plowing. I spend all day painting houses. I work in the kitchen all by myself. There is no way I can witness where I am. Is my work still meaningful?*

Absolutely. Remember Proverbs 14:23a: "In all labor there is profit"? Daniel's job was a secular one, an ordinary job. He was a government bureaucrat. And I am sure that as Daniel was handling taxation, administration, public relations, law enforcement, building projects, meetings, and diplomacy, he'd implore, "What does this have to do with serving God?" Yet, he served God continually.

Let me ask you a question. Who was the first farmer? Think about it. If you answered Adam you would be wrong. You can find it in Genesis 2:8a: "And the LORD God planted a garden eastward in Eden." The first farmer was God, and that tells me farming is an honorable occupation.

So God planted the first garden, and then He turned it over to Adam. "Then the LORD God took the man and put him in the Garden of Eden to tend and keep it" (Genesis 2:15).

Never have the idea that work is the punishment for sin. God gave Adam work to do before he sinned. God made Adam part caretaker of this world. Why a garden? Because people have to eat.

The home of Jesus was the cottage of a working man. And Jesus, whether He was mending plows or mending souls, was doing the work of God. People have to have houses to live in, furniture to sit on, food to eat, and clothes to wear. And when we are doing those things we are participating with God, and cooperating with God, as much as Adam was when he was taking care of the garden that God had planted.

This is my Father's world. Away with the idea that the material world is wrong or out of whack with God. God made these things, and He knows they have to operate, or we could not have humanity; we could not have life.

Ephesians 6:7-8 says, "With goodwill doing service, as to the Lord, and not to men, knowing that whatever good thing anyone does, he will receive the same from the Lord, whether he is a slave or free."

That means if you are a slave, having absolutely no choice about what you are doing, if you still do it with a smile on your face and a song in your heart, Jesus will reward you.

Isn't that beautiful? That puts dignity in your work. And regardless of what that job is, you should go to work tomorrow with a song in your heart, a smile on your face, and a spring in your step.

And if you are putting those tops on tubes of toothpaste, pray, "This one is for you, Jesus." And send it on down the line. Nobody else but you will know about it. Isn't that wonderful?

You see, every day is a holy day. And every place is a sacred place. Again, "And whatever you do, do it heartily, as to the Lord and not to men, knowing that from the Lord you shall receive the reward of the inheritance: for you serve the Lord Christ" (Colossians 3:23-24). Don't get so heavenly minded you are no earthly good. God has you right where you are to do a job.

There were some people who, when they were taken out of Israel and put in Babylon, just sat down and protested, "This is a decadent society. It's an ungodly world. I'm not going to work in it. I'm not going to participate in it."

But I want you to see what Jeremiah told them:

> Thus says the LORD of hosts, the God of Israel, to all who are carried away captive, whom I have caused to be carried away from Jerusalem to Babylon; Build houses and dwell in them; plant gardens and eat their fruit. Take wives and beget sons and daughters; and take wives for your sons and give your daughters to husbands, so that they may bear sons and daughters - that you may be increased there, and not diminished. And seek the peace of the city where I have caused you to be carried away captive, and pray to the LORD for it: for in its peace you will have peace. (Jeremiah 29:4-7)

As Christians we are to look for a city without foundations whose builder and maker is God. But while we are here we are to seek the good of the city in which we live. God wants us to make the city where we are a better place to live. Because in its peace we will have peace.

Every place is a sacred place. Every day is a holy day. You are a priest of God, a minister of God in full-time Christian service. If that doesn't ring your bell, your clapper is broken. That will make a difference when you go out tomorrow.

"In all labor there is profit."

CHAPTER ELEVEN

THE PERIL OF PRIDE

These six things the LORD hates, Yes, seven are an abomination to Him: A proud look, a lying tongue, hands that shed innocent blood, a heart that devises wicked plans, feet that are swift in running to evil, a false witness that speaks lies, and one who sows discord among brethren.
(Proverbs 6:16-19)

P ride is dangerous and deadly. I know of nothing that is doing more to...

dam the floodgates of revival,
damn and doom our nation,
destroy our homes,
devastate lives,
drain power from Christians, and
domicile the place called hell...

...than the damaging, disastrous sin of pride! But it is such a deceptive sin. The people who are the proudest least admit their pride. As a matter of fact, they are quite "proud of their humility." And many have pride that is well-hidden, but it is there nonetheless.

One fellow remarked to a friend, "At least I don't have any difficulty with the sin of pride."

And his friend replied, "Well, why should you have any difficulty with pride? You have nothing to be proud of!"

"Oh yeah," the man boasted, "I have as much to be proud of as you do!"

Pride is incipient in all of us. What a deceitful sin it is! But we must understand what pride is not, because we call many things pride, and we often use the word "pride" to describe things that are not really pride from a biblical standpoint.

Self-esteem is not pride. You need it; you ought to have it. When you understand who you are in Christ, you will realize that God gives you a good self-image. The grace of God exalts a person without inflating him and debases him without humiliating him. And, therefore, pride is not found in a good self-image.

Neither is pride the rejoicing in honor given. Athletes are not necessarily proud in the bad sense of the word when they win gold medals and trophies. Most have a sense of gratefulness and a sense of achievement. That is not the kind of pride the Bible condemns.

As a matter of fact, the Bible speaks of giving honor to whom honor is due. And if the Bible commends us for honoring others, then it is certainly not sinful for us to receive honor when it is due and warranted.

A man is to honor his wife. "Husbands, likewise, dwell with them with understanding, giving honor to the wife" (1 Peter 3:7a). So, when a man says to his wife, "Honey, I'm proud of you"—he is giving her honor, that is the emphatic teaching of God's Word.

The Bible further states: "Nevertheless let every one of you in particular so love his wife as himself, and let the wife see that she respects her husband" (Ephesians 5:33). Wife, you are to reverence, honor, and respect your husband. You ought to say, "Dear, I'm proud of you." You ought to give him a pat on the back. That's all many a husband needs.

A woman is to a man what a wind is to a fire. She can fan up a man's enthusiasm or blow it out. Wives, we husbands need for you to encourage us. That is one reason God gave you to us.

It is good to encourage people. That is why Barnabas is in the New Testament. He was such a helper and encourager and saw the best in his Christian brethren, that they called him "Barnabas" (not his real name that was Joseph), which means "encourager." Sometimes it helps for us to hear, "I'm proud of you." Conversely, we ought to say, from time to time, "I'm proud of you."

I heard about a couple that had been married for about sixty years. They were sitting in front of a fire, and the elderly husband had a romantic twinge. Turning to look at his spouse of six decades, he exulted, "I'm proud of you." She was hard of hearing and asked, "Ehh?" He repeated, "I'm proud of you!" "Ehh?" He finally yelled, "I'M PROUD OF YOU!" She responded, "Yeah, and I'm tired of you, too!"

That didn't work out too well, but under normal circumstances it is praiseworthy to tell someone you are proud of them. It is worthwhile to give them honor.

When the Bible warns against pride, it does not warn against the satisfaction of a job well done. One ought to do his work with pride. If you are sweeping the floor, you ought not miss the corners. Colossians 3:23 says, "And whatever you do, do it heartily, as to the Lord and not to men."

When you dress you ought to dress nicely. Going around looking like an unmade bed does not mean you are humble. That's not a sign of humility—that's just sloppiness.

There is a good, healthy self-respect the Bible does not condemn. Rather, the Bible encourages it. When I refer to pride I am not talking about self-respect, conscientiousness, or receiving proper honor.

What is this sin called pride that the Bible so vigorously condemns?

Number one, it is an attitude of independence from God. It is saying, "God, I don't need You. I can do it myself. I can manage my own life, thank You."

The agnostic William Ernest Henley wrote, "I am the master of my fate, I am the captain of my soul." I feel like answering, "Captain, your ship is about to sink!" But all around us are those who feel they are self-sufficient without God. And that self-sufficiency, that arrogant spirit of independence apart from God, is what the Bible calls pride.

That independence results in a sense of ingratitude, which is also one of the facets of pride. When a person has a base and ungrateful spirit, he is proud. Why? Because he does not acknowledge the God who has given him all he has.

Pride is what the Bible calls this attitude of ingratitude. It causes us, then to measure ourselves by one another, to esteem ourselves better than others. All of this is a matter of pride.

Let me narrow the scope a bit more and give you certain tests or indications of pride.

- Does it irritate you when someone corrects you for your faults?
- Do you find yourself accepting praise for things over which you have no control? That is, for natural abilities and gifts God has given you? Yet you receive the praise as unto yourself, rather than acknowledging the God who gave you that ability and passing the praise on to Him. If you receive the praise, then you are proud.
- Are you an individual who, when he does make a mistake, always has an alibi? Always has an excuse? Always justifies that mistake and brushes it off? That is a situation of pride.
- When someone wrongs you or does something you dislike, do you ever rationalize, "Well, I can get along without that individual. I don't need him"? Your sense of self-sufficiency, not needing and not wanting the other person, is pride.
- Do you find it difficult to seek counsel, to ask someone else for advice? Are you the type of individual who brags, "I don't need anybody to tell me what to do"? My wife Joyce says, "Adrian, you don't even like to drive into a service station and ask directions." That's true. I simply want to figure it out for myself. And I have to admit it, if it were anybody else, that would be a form of pride. Ahem!
- Do you have an ungrateful spirit, not accepting graciously what God has given you? Or perhaps grumbling for what God has not given you, as though He owes you? That's pride.
- Is your life marked by a sense of competition? Do you measure success by victory over other people? Pride is not merely wanting more for yourself—it is wanting more than someone else has. And sometimes it is wanting to have everything for yourself and nothing for anyone else. This sense of competition reveals that we think somehow we must win, that we inherently deserve more, or we are better than someone else.

All of the preceding are indications of pride, that spirit of independence from God, of ingratitude, of competition that causes us to think of ourselves as somehow better than others. *And God hates it!*

In the book of Proverbs I want us to look at five things pride does. Then I want us to see how we can deal with the arrogant, heinous sin of pride.

PRIDE PROVOKES DEITY

Pride angers God. That should make every conscientious person shiver. Look in Proverbs 6:16-17. "These six things the LORD hates: Yes, seven are an abomination to Him: a proud look..." According to this, you can sin even by the way you look. Some people can strut sitting down. God hates it.

Proverbs 16:5a says the same thing: "Everyone proud in heart is an abomination to the LORD." Why does God have this intense antipathy, this hatred, this abhorrence of pride?

Pride Made The Devil

It is because of what pride does. If there had been no pride, there would have been no devil. It was pride that made the devil—the devil.

To begin with, the devil was the most glorious being God ever created. The Bible records that he was full of wisdom and beauty. God has never made a creature more exquisitely beautiful, more wise, more powerful than Lucifer, "the son of the morning."

His very name, Lucifer, means "light-bearer." And the book of Ezekiel says that he was perfect in all of his ways "till iniquity was found in [him]" (see 28:12-19).

And that iniquity was pride. The Bible makes this clear. First Timothy 3:6 gives qualifications for someone who would like to be a preacher: "Not a novice, lest being lifted up with pride he fall into the condemnation of the devil."

That is, if you ordain a man who is inexperienced and immature, he may become proud. And that pride may cause the same thing to happen to him that pride caused to happen to the devil. I repeat: pride made the devil—the devil. Pride corrupted the most glorious creature God ever created.

Pride Ruined The Race

Not only was it pride that made the devil—the devil, *but it was pride that ruined the race.* What was the bait the devil used when he seduced Eve? It was this: "You will be like God. You will know as much as God" (see Genesis 3:4-5). What a lie!

Eve would never have done what she did just for a bite of fruit. It was more than the tantalizing taste or the appetizing appearance or the fragrant aroma. Behind what she did was a tremendous pull, a crushing pressure. The devil appealed to her and put pride in her heart, claiming, "You can be like the Most High God."

Pride Ushered Sin Into The World

Pride, therefore, ruined the race—and because of that, *pride ushered sin into the world.* Every rape, every murder, every act of pillage, every shred of dishonesty, every kind of cruelty, every type of perversion is caused by pride. All suffering, all sorrow, all sin is the result of pride.

No pride, no devil. No devil, no fall. No fall, no sin. It is all rooted in pride. This is the reason the Bible declares, "These six things the LORD hates: Yes, seven are an abomination to Him." *And number one on that list is a proud look.*

All of the other six crawl like snakes from the first one. Pride leads the parade. It is the basic sin that leads to all other sins. It is the sin of independence from God. It is wrapped up in our believing God. But why do people not believe God? Because they think they know a better way, which is indeed pride at its worst.

And so I want you to recognize that *pride provokes Deity.* Man's pride strikes at the very heart of God. Pride disbelieves God with blatant unbelief. Pride, in essence, calls God Almighty a bearer of falsehoods, rather than recognizing that God is "true and every man a liar" (see Romans 3:4), as Paul put it. Pride, in its most brazen form, rebels against Deity, flies in the face of His righteousness, thumbs its nose at holiness, laughs and mocks at the Godhead.

People provoke God to anger when pride is in their hearts. God will not help you in your pride but literally will become your adversary, your opponent, and your enemy if you hang onto pride. The Bible says, "God resists the proud" (James 4:6b). God rises and calls the entire universe against the proud person.

PRIDE PROVES DEPRAVITY

Sometimes people do not think they are sinners because, "They don't cuss, and they don't chew, and they don't go with the girls who do." They claim, "I'm all right. I don't do this. I don't do that. I don't steal. I don't lie. I don't murder. I don't commit adultery."

And many people are like that, but they have an overriding sin that is worse than all of that: pride in their hearts. Center on Proverbs 16:5a again: "Everyone proud in heart is an abomination to the LORD."

That is exactly where pride can be found—in the heart. It never has to reach the hands or the feet. Pride in the heart is an abomination to the Lord.

Key in on Proverbs 21:4: "A haughty look, a proud heart, and the plowing of the wicked are sin." That is an amazing verse. What do these have to do with one another? Think of a farmer who does not acknowledge God, because he feels self-sufficient. Can you imagine anyone so dependent on God's sun and rain and soil being so independent? He boasts, "I don't need God." So he goes out and plows his field.

No, he is not robbing a bank. He is not committing adultery. He is not practicing sodomy. He is not beating his wife. He is just plowing a field—that is all—but the Bible observes that even "the plowing of the wicked, is sin."

Why? Because the wicked farmer has a proud heart. And because of that, all he touches, he contaminates. The farmer who does not acknowledge the Source of the rain and the soil and the sun, and does not confess that God causes that seed to grow, and does not believe he is absolutely, utterly dependent upon God, is a proud man. So, even when he plows his field, he is sinning before God.

Many people's greatest need is to *see their need*. They don't realize that when God looks at a person, God doesn't look as people do. "For the LORD does not see as man sees; for man looks at the outward appearance, but the LORD looks at the heart" (1 Samuel 16:7b). That pride in the heart proves depravity.

How did that pride get into the heart? If you have an apple and that apple has a wormhole in it, you might think, *I better be careful. There is a worm in this apple.*

No, there is no worm in that apple. The hole is not there so the worm could get in; it is there so the worm could get out! The worm did not bore into that apple; the worm bore his way out of that apple. The worm, you see, was already in the apple.

You may argue, "Now wait a minute. How did the worm get into the apple?" It was born in the apple—that is how. He was hatched in the apple. The egg was laid in the apple blossom; the apple blossom became an apple; and that worm was on the inside. He simply ate his way out.

And the pride in your heart is there because it was born in your heart. When the worm of pride comes out to the surface, it is because it was already there in your heart.

Jesus taught in Mark 7:15: "There is nothing that enters a man, from outside which can defile him; but the things which come out of him, those are the things that defile a man." It is not the worm that bores into a man. And then Jesus added, "For from within, out of the heart of men, proceed...pride" (Mark 7:21a, 22b).

We are all born, as children of Adam and Eve, with a predisposition to sin. We are born egotists, which is another word for prideful, sinful beings. We are born self-centered.

If you don't believe me, then try giving a little child a sack full of candy, more than he could possibly eat. And then ask the child, "Now that I've given you that candy, can I have a piece?" That baby will protest, "No, it's mine!" Isn't that right? That's the inborn selfishness of a child.

When you were a little child there in the nursery, this may have happened to you. You were surrounded with fifteen toys, yet you were playing with only one of them, not caring at all about the other toys. And then someone came to visit your mother and put another baby on the floor with you. And that other baby went over and picked up one of those toys you weren't playing with.

You left your one toy, took another toy, bopped that baby on the head with it, and then snatched that one toy away from him, because you did not want him to have that toy. You wanted them all for yourself. Right?

You see, pride is born in the heart of a person, like the worm in the heart of the apple. It comes to the surface. When it does, it proves our depravity. There is not a mother's child who is not born egocentric. We do not learn pride; we inherit it.

You don't have to teach a child to be selfish. No one has ever taught a child to be that way. You have to teach a child not to be selfish. By nature we are selfish, self-centered, and self-seeking. By nature we all come into this world wanting to be our own little god, sitting upon the throne of our own little lives, worshiping at the shrine of our own egos.

PRIDE PROMOTES DISSENSION

There has never been a war, never been a fight, never been a scuffle, unless it was rooted in pride. Proverbs 13:10a tells us: "*By* pride comes nothing but strife" (italics mine).

Every war was begun with pride as a major factor. Every church split has pride behind it somewhere. Every divorce occurs because pride is involved. Every argument is caused somehow by pride.

You ask, "Are you certain?" That's what the Bible says. "By pride comes nothing but strife." But you *contend*, "Well, no, we had genuine problems that weren't really caused by pride." I'm not saying you didn't have problems. I'm saying it was pride that kept you from solving those problems.

There are no problems too big to solve, only people too small to solve them. The reason husbands and wives have arguments is that they do not attack the problem—they attack each other. Ego against ego. "By pride comes nothing but strife."

Those problems can be solved. What often happens in a marriage is that Mary and James (we will use those names) come to emotional, verbal, and/or physical blows early in their marriage. Mary, who has not given her heart to Christ, is egocentric. She was born wanting to be the queen who sits on the throne of her life. James is also—you guessed it—egocentric. He is self-centered, selfish, and full of pride. He was born wanting to be king in his own little kingdom.

So we are confronted with Queen Mary and King James! They have moved into an apartment, a mobile home, or even a house. But there is a problem. They have two kingdoms under one roof. And Jesus plainly declared, "A house divided against itself will not stand" (Matthew 12:25b).

Before long there will be war between those two kingdoms. It may be a "cold war" with neither of them speaking, or it may be a "hot war" with Mary throwing a frying pan or James using his fist. After a while a tragedy called divorce occurs. Dreadfully tragic. And behind it all is... PRIDE.

Suppose, though, that it had gone differently. Let's pretend that one day Mary became convicted of her sin, aware of her pride and her selfishness. Not that she was a terrible person, not that she was a horrible adulteress, not that she was a sneaky thief—but she simply realized that she was woefully self-centered instead of God-centered. Rather than seeking God's glory, she had sought glory for Queen Mary.

And, repenting of her sins, she dethroned self and enthroned King Jesus Christ. She confessed, "Jesus, I recognize that You are Lord. You have every right to rule over my life. I yield my heart and my life to You. I want You to sit on the throne of my heart!" And suppose James had done the same—repented of his sin, received Christ, and then enthroned Him.

> *When self is on the throne, Christ is on the cross.*
> *When Christ is on the throne, self is on the cross.*

So, suppose both of them had enthroned Christ within their hearts. And Jesus Himself came into James and Mary through the precious Holy Spirit. Christ was actually living in them. "I have been crucified with Christ: it is no longer I who live, but Christ lives in me; and the life which I now live in the flesh I live by faith in the Son of God, who loved me and gave Himself for me" (Galatians 2:20).

Christ was dwelling in Mary and James, so the Jesus in Mary was not going to fight the Jesus in James, and the Jesus in James was not going to fight the Jesus in Mary. They no longer had two kingdoms. They had the same King residing in and ruling over them.

Now that didn't mean that Mary and James would never have any differences. I will admit that my dear wife Joyce and I have our share of differences. This is America—she has a right to be wrong! Just kidding! I'd hate to be married to someone I didn't differ with in some areas. How dull that would be.

If you always agree, one of you is not thinking. You will have differences, but if those differences are to be worked out, you must deal with pride. You attack the problem, not your loved one. Approaching your differences and difficulties, with Jesus on the throne, is exciting and exhilarating.

I repeat: "Only by pride cometh contention." The devil would rather start a church fuss than sell a carload of whiskey!

If churches would only stay humble before the Lord, and the members of those churches would be willing to subjugate themselves unto the Lordship of Christ, they would never have contention. They might have problems—but not contention.

Nail it down. Pride provokes Deity. It is an abomination to God because of what it does. Pride also proves depravity. When a person has pride in his heart, it is there because it was born in him. Jesus said, "It is what comes out of his heart that defiles him." Pride also produces dissension. If we are not right with God, it is no wonder that we cannot be right with one another.

PRIDE PROMOTES DISHONOR

Now this is ironic. Guess what the proud person wants. He wants the acclaim of other people. He craves honor.

As I have pointed out, there is nothing wrong with having honor, because the Bible indicates we are to give honor to whom honor is due (see Romans 13:7). God clearly teaches that He will honor those who honor Him. "For those who honor Me I will honor, and those who despise Me shall be lightly esteemed" (1 Samuel 2:30b).

But the sad irony is this: the proud man who desperately grasps for honor is the one who ultimately loses it. Proverbs 11:2a illustrates this truth: "When pride comes, then comes shame." As night follows day, shame follows pride.

Proverbs 15:33 reminds us that "The fear of the LORD is the instruction of wisdom, and before honor is humility." That verse instructs us how to have honor, so we know it is not wrong to be honored rightfully. But before honor is humility. On the other side, before shame is pride.

Pride produces dishonor. "Before destruction the heart of man is haughty, and before honor is humility" (Proverbs 18:12). God wants to make it plain, doesn't He? "A man's pride will bring him low, but the humble in spirit" will retain honor (Proverbs 29:23). God wants to remind us because we are so prone to forget. Pride never fosters honor—in the long run, only dishonor.

And yet people live so pridefully because they want the applause and plaudits of men. They lust after honor. And honor is the very thing they will never get!

Have you ever been around people who absolutely "reek" with conceit? Some astute observer has expressed it: "Conceit is a disease that makes everybody sick except the one who has it." But the conceited person is the sickest of all. Intoxicated with self-importance and blinded to his prideful sin, the conceited person thinks that by all of his pompous pride and attention-getting actions, he is somehow going to gain the admiration of people yet—he loses what he most wants, the honor of others.

Pride never issues in honor. It ushers in shame. It fosters and promotes dishonor.

Why? Because God has placed a fundamental rule in life: The way up is down. Jesus taught: "But he who is greatest among you shall be your servant. And whoever exalts himself will be humbles [brought low], and he who humbles himself will be exalted" (Matthew 23:11-12). This is a basic principle God has set in motion.

A prime example of this is found in Isaiah 14. God asked a rhetorical question. How did the devil become the devil? Here it is: "How you are fallen from heaven, O Lucifer, son of the morning! How you are cut down to the ground, you who weakened the nations!" (v. 12).

God was asking Satan "What has happened to you? What has made you what you are?" And He answers His rhetorical question in verses 13 and 14. "For you have said in your heart: I will ascend into heaven, I will exalt my throne above the stars of God; I will also sit on the mount of the congregation on the farthest sides of the north; I will ascend above the heights of the clouds, I will be like the Most High."

Satan was proud. He boasted, "I'm too beautiful, I'm too wise, I'm too cunning, I'm too strong, I'm too mighty to be anything less than God. I'm going to be like God. I'm going to be like the Most High." He exalted himself.

What was he seeking? Praise, admiration, adulation, fame, and honor. But let us continue in this text. Put a circle around the word "yet" in verse 15. "Yet you shall be brought down to Sheol, to the lowest depths of the Pit." Satan boasted, "I'm going to go as high as You can go." To which God replied, "No, you are going as low as one can go."

Verses 16-17: "Those who see you will gaze at you, and consider you, saying, Is this the man that made the earth tremble, who shook kingdoms, who made the world as a wilderness and destroyed its cities, who did not open the house of his prisoners?"

What does this mean? One day, in the ages to come, the devil will be put on exhibit. All of the saints of the ages, and all of the created hosts are going to be the spectators. And God is going to ask, "Come over here. I want to show you something. Look down there."

And down in the pit, squirming like a worm in hot coals, in humiliation, in shame, in ignominious defeat, will be the devil, Lucifer, the son of the morning. Imagine it. The world quaked before him. "That old serpent"—that arrogant, rebellious fallen angel—who caused so much degradation and destruction will be writhing in the pit.

When we view that vanquished devil and all of his hellish hordes, and when we see what is going to happen to him, we will say, "You mean that's him? That's the devil? The one who made the nations tremble? That pitiful creature down there? The lowest of the low? That's the devil? That's Satan?"

Yes, that is he. *Pride brings shame.* We will behold Satan in his humiliation and shame. Satan pompously said, "I will ascend." On the other hand there was One who propitiously said, "I will descend."

> Let this mind be in you which was also in Christ Jesus, who, being in the form of God, did not consider it robbery to be equal with God, but made Himself of no reputation, taking on Him the form of a bondservant, and coming in the likeness of men. And being found in appearance as a man, He humbled Himself and became obedient to the point of death, even the death of the cross. Therefore God also has highly exalted Him and given Him the name which is above every name, that at the name of Jesus every knee should bow, of those in heaven, and of those on the earth, and of those under the earth, and that every tongue should confess that Jesus Christ is Lord, to the glory of God the Father. (Philippians 2:5-11)

You are called to decide which lifestyle to follow. You can follow the prideful way of the devil. That way seems to be up, but it is down. You can take the way of the Lord Jesus Christ, the way of genuine humility and true humility. To the world that way seems to be down, but it is up, up, up.

Pride produces dishonor. You can strut now if you want. It seems most of the people in America are egomaniacs strutting their way to hell, thinking they are too good to be damned.

Pride will bring you low. It always has. It always will. That leads us to the fact that...

PRIDE PRECEDES DESTRUCTION

The LORD will destroy the house of the proud. (Proverbs 15:25a)

Pride goes before destruction, and an haughty spirit before a fall. (Proverbs 16:18)

Before destruction the heart of a man is haughty. (Proverbs 18:12a)

These verses have a common thread—pride precedes destruction. People outside of Christ are not merely going to be humiliated—they are ultimately going to be destroyed. And that destruction does not mean annihilation, as some cultists falsely believe. It means everlasting punishment in a place the Bible calls hell. It means to be there with the devil and his angels for all of never-ending eternity.

Why? Because God hates pride, and God resists the proud. God sets Himself in battle array against the proud. Hell is the abode of the proud. "But the cowardly, unbelieving, abominable, murderers, sexually immoral people, sorcerers, idolaters, and all liars shall have their part in the lake which burns with fire and brimstone, which is the second death" (Revelation 21:8). Pride is behind all of the sinners in that verse of Scripture. Pride.

Pride Produces National Ruin

Our nation will come to naught unless we repent. God is looking for the repentance of humiliation. For He says, "If My people who are called by My name will humble themselves, and pray, and seek My face, and turn from their wicked ways, then I will hear from heaven, and will forgive their sin and heal their land" (2 Chronicles 7:14).

Pride Produces Domestic Ruin

Homes become battlegrounds because of pride. The divorce courts are full because of pride and because husbands and wives attack each other instead of their problems.

Pride Produces Financial Ruin

Many are in financial bondage because of pride. Marriage counselors, judges, and statisticians tell us that there are more divorces over finances than sex or children. Many families are buying items they don't need with money they don't have to impress people they don't like. Covetous pride is behind it. Our neighbors keep buying things we can't afford. Right? And we are trying to keep up with the Joneses and Smiths and Jablonskis and others. And many not only want to keep up with their neighbors, but to surpass them—all the way to bankruptcy court.

Pride Produces Emotional Ruin

Pride can ruin you emotionally if you spend considerable time worrying about what other people think. After all, you want to be "in." You shop at the "in" stores, wear the "in" shoes, play at the "in" golf course, or drive the "in" car. You have to judge everything as to whether it is "state of the art."

Pride can make one's life a nightmare of unnecessary trivia that has nothing to do with success from the standpoint of God's Word. To me one of the most vacuous pursuits in America is publishing lists of "ins" and "outs." Who cares? But pride dictates those "ins" and "outs" and tries to tell people what is acceptable. This whole status game is a subtle form of slavery that can never be satisfied. It will ruin and wreck a person emotionally until he is tied in a thousand knots of unnecessary protocol. Pride has made him a slave to opinion.

Pride Produces Eternal Ruin

Worst of all, hell will be packed with prideful people who thought they had no need of God and that they could make it apart from Him.

Jesus spoke about two contrasting men who "went up to the temple to pray" (Luke 18:10a)—one a Pharisee and the other a tax collector. The Pharisee was a self-righteous person, but his religion was only a cosmetic that covered a hard, hateful, prideful heart.

The Pharisee stood and prayed thus with himself [the indication is that the prayer ended up being to himself]. "God, I thank You that I am not like other men - extortioners, unjust, adulterers, or even as this tax collector. I fast twice in the week, I give tithes of all I possess" (Luke 18:11-12).

He pointed the finger of accusation at the tax collector, the hated tax collector who was "standing afar off." The Pharisee strutted like a plump peacock in the face of God.

But the poor tax collector, a sinner who was painfully aware of his sin, beat himself upon the chest, which was a Middle Eastern gesture of humiliation and deep remorse. "And the tax collector, standing afar off, would not so much as raise his eyes unto heaven, but beat his breast, saying, 'God be merciful to me a sinner!'" (Luke 18:13). Literally, the Greek should be translated, "God mercy me the sinner." That is right. "Mercy me."

In other words, "Apply Your mercy to me." And there is the literal "mercy me *the* sinner." The *sinner*. When a person is under profound conviction of the Holy Spirit, he feels as if he is the only sinner on the face of the earth, "the sinner," "the chief of sinners," as Paul testified he was (see 1 Timothy 1:15). The publican recognized that he was the sinner of sinners.

What was the outcome? "I tell you," Jesus explained, "this man [the tax collector] went down to his house justified rather than the other; for everyone who exalts himself will be humble,; and he who humbles himself will be exalted" (Luke 18:14).

Two men went home from church that day. One, the Pharisee, went home dignified. The other, the publican, went home justified, saved, forgiven, redeemed, born again.

The devil will whisper to you, "Hey, keep your dignity. Don't ever admit your need of the Lord," But until you admit your desperate need of the Lord, you will never be saved.

Perhaps you reply, "But, I'm not all that bad. I'm a pretty good person." But that's pride answering for you. Pride is a matter of the heart. The Pharisee pontificated, "Lord, I thank You that I am not as other men are." He was comparing himself with others. He should have had his eyes upon the Lord.

When Job saw the Lord he cried out, "I abhor myself" (Job 42:6a). When Isaiah saw the Lord he moaned, "Woe is me" (Isaiah 6:5a). When Peter saw the Lord he begged, "Depart from me, Lord, for I am a sinful man" (Luke 5:8b). When Daniel saw the Lord he confessed, "my vigor was turned to frailty" (Daniel 10:8b).

Isaac Watts caught the truth of which I am writing:

When I survey the wondrous cross,
On which the Prince of Glory died;
My richest gain I count but loss,
And pour contempt on all my pride.

Stop comparing yourself with other people and compare yourself with the Lord Jesus. There is none so bad he cannot be saved, and there is none so good he need not be saved.

The devil will goad you, "Don't you admit you have a need of God. Don't confess your sinnership. Stonewall it."

So many a sinner will walk away from God, bound in the chains of pride forged on the anvil of a hard heart. Some of you reading this are lost, unsaved, and you will probably stay lost and go to hell because you do not want to admit you have been a lost church member. You protest, "But what would people think?" You are so concerned with what people think. And it is pride that precedes destruction. "A haughty spirit goes before a fall."

Rather than admit your need before the Lord, rather than humble yourself before the Lord, you would choose spiritual destruction.

You might argue, "I'm not all that bad." Suppose it were possible to assemble the five billion-plus people currently living on earth. And then add to them all of the people who have died since Adam, and then compound that by all of the people who will yet come into being before time comes to an end. And if you were to put all of them in one place and extract from every one of those individuals their very best attributes, and then put all of those attributes into one man… that man would still have to kneel down and pray, "God be merciful to me a sinner."

The worst form of badness is human goodness, when that human goodness becomes a substitute for the new birth. The reason that some people are destroyed forever is because of pride. Pride seals one's doom and keeps him from believing in saving faith on the Lord Jesus.

"For everyone that exalts himself will be humbles, and he who humbles himself will be exalted." I pray you will come to the place in your life where you will pray, in the words of the human writer, "Lord, in my hand no price I bring, Simply to Your cross I cling."

Will you lay your spiritual and intellectual pride in the dust? Will you allow the humility engendered by the Holy Spirit to saturate your heart and life, so you can say, "Lord Jesus, I totally yield myself to You"?

CHAPTER TWELVE

WISDOM'S FINAL CALL

Wisdom calls aloud outside; she raises her voice in the open squares. She cries out in the chief concourses, at the openings of the gates in the city she speaks her words: How long, you simple ones, will you love simplicity? For scorners delight in their scorning, and fools hate knowledge. Turn at my rebuke; surely I will pour out my spirit on you; I will make my words known to you. Because I have called and you refused, I have stretched out my hand and no one regarded, because you distained all my counsel, and would have none of my rebuke, I also will laugh at your calamity; I will mock when your terror comes, when your terror comes like a storm, and your destruction comes like a whirlwind, when distress and anguish comes upon you. Then they will call on me, but I will not answer; they will seek me diligently; but they will not find me. Because they hated knowledge and did not choose the fear of the LORD, they would have none of my counsel and despised my every rebuke. Therefore they shall eat of the fruit of their own way, and be filled to the full with their own fancies. For the turning away of the simple will slay them, and the complacency of fools will destroy them; but whoever listens to me will dwell safely, and will be secure, without fear of evil.
(Proverbs 1:20-33)

Not long ago I had to catch an airplane to meet a pressing engagement. In other words, I seemed to be running late.

Sometimes I ought to have the sign: "The hurrier I go, the behinder I get." I weaved my way through the traffic, checked my bags, and hurried through the concourse. My trip was going to be long, my bags were heavy, and I began to worry about the old ticker. Fearing a heart attack I finally reached the gate, gave them my ticket, and picked up my boarding pass. Then I looked at the clock and realized, to my amazement, that I had plenty of time.

I thought, *Adrian, you desperately need to relax.* So I bought a newspaper and a cup of tea and sat there leisurely in the waiting room. After a while I looked up and thought, *Where did everybody go?* Nervous, I went to the attendant and asked, "When are you going to call this flight?" "Mister, it is called," he came back. So I inquired further, "Well, when is it going to leave?" "It left" was his succinct reply.

I was so dumb I sat right there in the waiting room, near the gate, heard the final call, and let that plane leave without me! (Confession is good for the soul.)

You may do something infinitely more foolish than that. You may sit in a church or listen to the Gospel on radio or television, right at the gates of glory, hear God make His final call, and let the last plane to heaven leave without you!

WISDOM'S INVITATION

Wisdom calls aloud outside; she raises her voice in the open squares. (Proverbs 1:20)

It Is A Public Invitation

Salvation is for every person, not only a select few. John wrote: "And He Himself is the propitiation for our sins, and not for ours only but also for the whole world" (1 John 2:2). Jesus died not only for those who have accepted Him but also for every man, woman, and child, regardless of their status. "The sins of the whole world."

Certain lodges and secret societies may require a member to go through an initiation in order for those societies to reveal their hidden wisdom. The initiate is not supposed to share that esoteric knowledge. Frankly, if it is so good, it ought to be shared and spread abroad. Jesus told His disciples, "in secret have I said nothing" (John 18:20).

Wisdom speaks openly, enthusiastically. I have often heard the expression, "Keep the faith." Not only should you keep it, you ought to give it away. If you do not have a desire to give it away, you ought to forget it, because what you have is not real, saving faith. Matthew 10:27b says, "What you hear in the ear, preach on the housetops."

It Is A Pressing Invitation

There is no "take-it-or-leave-it" attitude with wisdom. There is a sob in the throat and a tear in the voice of wisdom. There is an emergency and urgency. There is compassion and warning.

Sometimes people wonder why I stand in the pulpit week after week and plead "Come to Jesus, come to Jesus." Why? Because l am captivated and haunted by Paul's words: "Knowing, therefore, the terror of the Lord, we persuade men" (2 Corinthians 5:11a). This business of winning souls is a matter of life and death. I am not just playing church.

It Is A Patient Invitation

How long , you simple ones, will you love simplicity? For scorners delight in their scorning, and fools hate knowledge. (Proverbs 1:22)

Wisdom is patient with the simple and even with the scorner. Wisdom has even gone the second, third, and fourth miles with the fool. Wisdom stands with outstretched hands and laments, "How long, how long?" "The Lord is not slack [slow] concerning His promise, as some count slackness, but is longsuffering toward us, not willing that any should perish but that all should come to repentance" (2 Peter 3:9).

Through wisdom God has spoken to you repeatedly, and yet He may well be giving you another opportunity as He gently urges, "How long will it be?"

Proverbs 1:22 mentions three classes of people. We have dealt with them earlier—the simple, the scorner, and the fool. The simple (open, susceptible) is the person who accepts most anything and everything hook, line, and sinker. He seems to have no strong opinions or serious thoughts.

Proverbs 22:3, as we have seen, makes it plain that "A prudent man foresees evil, and hides himself, but the simple pass on and are punished." That is, they do not even sense the danger. They seem to think there is no death to die, no judgment to face, and no hell to shun. They are careless and lackadaisical.

Really, the believer sometimes wants to shake the simple. "Wake up. Get in the ball game. Don't you know what you're up against? Don't you know there is an eternity? Why do you live like that? Why can't you get concerned and serious?

As the old hymn goes, "Death is coming, hell is moving!" In the name of all that is holy and decent, in the light of the shed blood of the Lord Jesus Christ, please wake up!"

Once there was a baron in Germany who loved to play the violin. In those days it was common for nobility to have a chaplain. The chaplain had preached the Lord Jesus and His saving death over and over again to the baron.

The baron, caught up in his violin, would call together his staff, including the chaplain and the servants. During one of the baron's performances, the chaplain sat with a yawn and practically no expression on his face. Angered, the baron stopped his playing and shouted, "My good chaplain, have you no soul? Here I am pouring out my very soul through this instrument, and you sit there unmoved and bored. How dare you?"

"If it please your grace," replied the preacher, "For years I have ushered you to the door of heaven with the sweetest notes of the Gospel. I have played the entire scale of heaven's matchless music again and again and again, and day after day and year after year, you have sat unmoved by the sweetest music of the universe. How dare you reject the symphony of salvation?"

The simple may become the scorner—jesting and joking about the things of God. He then becomes the cynical. A person is not a sinner because he is a cynic; he is a cynic because he is a sinner.

Point out a man who laughs at holy things, and I'll show you one who has the devil's initials carved into his heart. Show me a woman who ridicules the things of God, and I'll show you one who is covered with the slimy fingerprints of sin. These people know the price of everything and the value of nothing. Yet, to them wisdom still speaks.

As I have explained in the chapter, "How Not to Raise a Fool," the final step in this dance of damnation is the fool. Simple, then scornful, then foolish. He is careless, then cynical, and finally callous.

A "fool" does not mean a person without mental equipment. Many a person with a high IQ has been a fool. A fool is someone, according to the book of Proverbs, who has chosen a lifestyle diametrically against God. He hates the knowledge and wisdom of God. The simple loves simplicity, the scorner delights in scorning, but the fool hates knowledge.

When a person is preoccupied with loving what he ought to hate, and vice versa, his judgment will become distorted and perverted. When this transformation occurs, he becomes what the Bible calls a fool.

Yet, amazingly enough, wisdom is still there. She is there with tears coursing down her cheeks, her lips bursting with a plea, her hands outstretched. Let me paraphrase the hymn of invitation: "Softly and tenderly, wisdom is calling; calling for you and for me... Calling, O sinner, come home!" Jesus is calling through wisdom. He is the embodiment of wisdom—the Logos. He is the Way, the Truth, and the Life (see John 14:6).

WISDOM'S INDOCTRINATION

Perhaps you are saying, "I can't help it if I don't believe. How can it be my fault if God doesn't speak to me?" But it is your own responsibility, for the one who does not hear the voice of wisdom is without excuse. "Turn you at my rebuke. surely I will pour out my spirit on you, I will make known my words to you" (Proverbs 1:23). Wisdom will reveal herself to anyone who will follow the three steps in this verse.

There Must Be The Repentance Of The Sinner

"Turn you at my rebuke." The word "turn" here is close to the idea of "repent" in the New Testament. It means to do a complete about-face, to change your mind, your intent, and your direction. "Let the wicked forsake his way, and the unrighteous man his thoughts; let him return to the LORD, and He will have mercy upon him; and to our God, for He will abundantly pardon" (Isaiah 55:7). But you must turn.

Wisdom never comes separate from repentance. Without repentance, God's Word would have the same effect on you as a drop of water on a boulder. Without repentance you are not able to receive and appropriate God's words.

There Will Be The Revelation Of The Spirit

I will pour out My spirit on you. (Proverbs 1:23b)

A Teacher has been given to you. He is the Holy Spirit. Even with a high IQ, you will never be able to begin understanding the Bible. Without the indwelling and enabling Holy Spirit, no one can appropriate the wealth of wisdom in the Word. You cannot lay gnarled and profane hands upon God's Holy Word and tear out the truths to stick into your mind.

"But the natural man does not receive the things of the Spirit of God, for they are foolishness to him; nor can he know them, because they are spiritually discerned" (1 Corinthians 2:14). Jesus said, "God has hid den these things from the wise and prudent and has revealed them to babes" (Luke 10:21a).

When a person repents, then God pours out His illuminating Spirit upon him and turns the light on in his soul. A babe in Christ can know infinitely more of God and His Word than a Rhodes scholar with five earned doctorates, if that scholar does not have Christ as his Savior.

There Is The Reliability Of The Scripture

I will make My words known to you. (Proverbs 1:23c)

For the LORD gives wisdom; from His mouth comes knowledge and understanding. He stores up sound wisdom for the uprightly. (Proverbs 2:6-7a)

The Holy Spirit is your Teacher, and the Bible is your Text, your Source. When you are saved, God laid up for you this vast wisdom in His Word, the Bible.

Count Tolstoy, the Christian novelist of Russia, wrote: "Without the Bible the education of the child in the present state of society is impossible." Andrew Jackson, during his last illness, declared that "the Bible is the rock on which our republic rests." William Lyon Phelps, famous preacher and educator, stated: "I believe a knowledge of the Bible without a college course is more valuable than a college course without a knowledge of the Bible."

When Sir Walter Scott, the brilliant Scottish writer, lay dying, he called to one of his servants, "Bring me the book." "What book, sir?" the servant asked. He replied, "My friend, there is only one Book—the Bible. Bring it to me!"

The Word of God is completely reliable. Jesus, the central Person of the Book, plainly taught the trustworthiness of the Word: "For assuredly, I say to you, till heaven and earth pass away, one jot or one tittle will by no pass from the law till all is fulfilled" (Matthew 5:18).

Jesus spoke to His detractors, "You search the Scriptures, for in them you think you have eternal life; and these are they which testify of Me" (John 5:39). Remember, He was speaking to the Jews, the scribes, and the Pharisees. They were unregenerate and thought they had salvation in the law and the prophets. Born-again believers are saved by the blood of Christ and know that the Word of God is totally true. Jesus said, "They testify of Me. The Scriptures bear record of Me."

WISDOM'S INDIGNATION

> Because I have called and you refused, I have stretched out
> my hand and no one regarded. (Proverbs 1:24)

Many verses treat the indignation of God. "Who can stand before His indignation?" (Nahum 1:6a). "But a certain fearful expectation of judgment, and fiery indignation which will devour the adversaries" (Hebrews 10:27).

Wisdom is patient, but did you realize you can so insult God's holiness that even His patience will come to an end? One of these days wisdom will make her final call. "And the LORD said, 'My Spirit shall not strive with man forever'" (Genesis 6:3a).

You can say no to God. Now, hyper-Calvinists have what they call the doctrine of limited atonement and irresistible grace. They claim that if God calls, you cannot refuse, and if He does not call, there is nothing you can do about it.

Do not believe it! Such a belief is the death knell to missions, evangelism, and soul-winning. More importantly, such is not taught in the Word of God. Dear friend, God calls and man often answers "no."

Jesus gazed down from the Mount of Olives upon the Holy City, Jerusalem, which would reap the bitter harvest of rejecting Him. With salty tears sweeping down His face, and a quiver in His voice, He cried, "O Jerusalem, Jerusalem, the one who kills the prophets and stones those who are sent to her! How often I have wanted to gather your children together, as a hen gathers her chicks under her wings, but you were not willing!" (Matthew 23:37).

It was not that Jerusalem's citizens *could* not—it was that they *would* not. Here I call to mind verses I have already used: "The Lord is not slack concerning His promise, as some men count slackness, but is longsuffering towards us, not willing that any should perish but that all should come to repentance" (2 Peter 3:9).

"[Christ] was the true Light which gives light to every man coming into the world" (John 1:9). "[Jesus] is the propitiation for our sins, and not for ours only but also for the whole world" (1 John 2:2). I'm everlastingly joyous that I can shout, "Whoever will may come."

But "whoever will" can refuse. You can choose to answer "no," of course. When that happens, invitation can turn to indignation. What will happen then?

There Will Be The Derision Of The Sinner

I also will laugh at your calamity; I will mock when your terror comes" (Proverbs 1:26).

The Scripture makes it clear that God is not mocked, "for whatever a man sows, that he will also reap" (Galatians 6:7). This is not the laugh of humor. God does not think it is funny. Here is the laughter of irony and absurdity.

You see, God has the last laugh. God is exercising His retribution. He has literally pled with you to receive His mercy. But even God will come to the end of His patience. He will remind the unrepentant sinner: "You mocked Me. I gave you every opportunity. You laughed at Me. Now that laughter has boomeranged and come back on your own head. You are reaping what you have sown. Your crop of foolishness and scorn is coming in. I will love you forever, but there was nothing I could do because you would not let Me."

There Will Be The Desolation Of The Sinner

When your fear cometh as desolation... (Proverbs 1:27a, KJV)

Desolation has a haunting, hollow sound to it. It is bone-chilling. It is kin to its ghastly cousins *lost, estranged, abandoned, reprobate.*

Three times in Romans 1 the Bible says, "God also gave them up," "God gave them up," and "God gave them over" (vv. 24, 26, 28).

If you are reading this, no doubt God's Spirit is speaking with you. At this moment, wisdom is calling you. I remind you: "God's Spirit shall not always strive with man." One of these days you could be left desolate.

Many a sensitive child was once under the compelling conviction of the Holy Ghost, but scorn entered in, tarnishing his pliable simplicity. Once that simple one cared, trembled at the thought of hell and judgment, and weighed the prospects of fleeing to Jesus. That simple one has become either a scorner, even worse, a fool in the worst sense. But there is no turning back the pages of time to that sensitive, almost naive, impressionable day when salvation and eternal life were so close at hand.

Polls have repeatedly cited the fact that Americans fear loneliness. Many do not want to live alone or die alone. But, contrary to the popular misconceptions, hell will be a forsaken, lonely place. There is no substantiation for the "good ole boy" notion that one will have all his gambling, beer-drinking buddies in hell.

Consider the rich man who lifted up his eyes in hell (see Luke 16:19-31). Even though he could somehow gaze across and view Lazarus, the poor beggar in Abraham's bosom, there is no indication the rich man was surrounded by company. Yes, multiplied hordes of the damned are there, but there is not one shred of proof that they communicate or lend any comfort to one another.

Do you better understand why I plead for people to be reconciled to God through the Lord Jesus Christ? How terrible it would be for you to be deaf to the voice of God and blind to His outstretched hands.

There Will Be The Destruction Of The Sinner

> And your destruction comes like a whirlwind; when distress and anguish come upon you. (Proverbs 1:27b)

Surely as night follows day, destruction will fall upon those who refuse to repent. As a cyclone or a hurricane, the biting, blasting, churning, destructive power will sweep away those who have refused Christ, and who can stand against it? The scorner and the fool will be devastated. Not annihilated but turned into hell, existing in a form of "living death" throughout eternity. Spiritually dead but existing in hell. No wonder the rich man did not want his brothers to end up in the pit!

Proverbs 29:1 warns: "He who is often rebuked. and hardens his neck, will suddenly be destroyed, and that without remedy." You have no idea when it will happen. Death lurks behind every bush, behind every parked car. This could be your last call.

> Then they will call on me, but I will not answer; they will seek me diligently, but they will not find me. Because they hated knowledge, and did not choose the fear of the LORD, they would have none of my counsel and despised my every rebuke. Therefore they shall eat the fruit of their own way, and be filled with their own fancies. (Proverbs 1:28-31)

Oh, how desperately they will plead! They will be like the drowning people in Noah's day. They scoffed at the preaching of Noah—laughing and mocking him. But, when the rain began to pour from above, and "the great fountains of the deep" were broken up from below, the scoffers yelled bloody murder as they beat on the sides of the ark. "Noah, have mercy!" But God had shut the door. They called, but it was too late.

Is God a God of grace and mercy and forgiveness? Yes! Every drop of Jesus' blood on Calvary's cross eloquently cries out, "God so loved the world, that He gave His only begotten Son" (John 3:16a). Gave His only begotten Son for you. May you be saved? Yes, if you want Jesus to enter your heart. But there is a deadline. There is a point at which mercy stops and judgment begins. It is too late then. There is no mercy at the Great White Throne of Judgment.

If you have the slightest desire to accept Christ, by all means do it now while there is the wooing of the Holy Spirit! Years ago I heard about one of the founding fathers of our nation. His granddaughter visited him at his country estate for the weekend, and she asked him, "Grandfather, they are having 'the protracted meeting' down at the church house, and I would like to go. Would you go with me?"

The old man looked out the window over his verdant fields and answered, "Dear, many years ago I was like you. I was young and sensitive like you. But I turned away from the calling of God. Now I no longer care. Dear, you go on to the meeting and make your profession of faith. The die is cast about my life."

If you want mercy, you may have it, provided the Holy Spirit is wooing you. But if you continue without Christ, you will come to a place of desperation where it will do you no good to throw yourself upon the mercy of the court. If you answer no to the God of grace, one day the God of judgment will answer no to you.

When the final call is sounded, answer. You are at the gate. Your boarding pass is available through Jesus' sacrifice. "Jesus paid it all." All you need do is answer yes instead of no. "Jesus, I am boarding right now. I want to be with You."

Fanny L. Crosby, the blind poet on earth but now sighted in heaven, wrote these pleading words:

> Jesus is tenderly calling you home,
> Calling today, calling today;
> Why from the sunshine of love will you roam
> Farther and farther away?
>
> Jesus is calling the weary to rest,
> Calling today, calling today;
> Bring Him your burden and you shall be blest;
> He will not turn You away.
>
> Jesus is waiting, O come to Him now,
> Waiting today, waiting today;
> Come with your sins; at His feet lowly bow;
> Come, and no longer delay.
>
> Jesus is pleading; O hear now His voice,
> Hear Him today, hear Him today;
> They who believe on His name shall rejoice;
> Quickly arise and away.
>
> Calling today, Calling today,
> Jesus is calling,
> Is tenderly calling today.

CPSIA information can be obtained
at www.ICGtesting.com
Printed in the USA
LVHW031929241121
704302LV00003B/7